PRAISE FOR TI AND JOHN HOLMES

"The Devil and John Holmes" is one of the most terrific sagas we have ever published."

—Jann Wenner, editor and publisher, *Rolling Stone*

"I can recongnize the truth in these stories—tales about the darkest possible side of wretched humanity. Sager has obviously spent too much time in flop houses in Laurel Canyon."

—Hunter S. Thompson, author of *Fear and Loathing in Las Vegas* and *Hells Angels*

"In his audio commentary on the New Line DVD release of '*Boogie Nights*,' P.T. Anderson cites as a major influence reporter Mike Sager's article in the June 15. 1989 *Rolling Stone*, 'The Devil and John Holmes'."

—Stephen Lemons, *Salon.com*

PRAISE FOR MIKE SAGER

"Sager takes us inside different worlds in a way that is immediate, vivid, and dramatic. He doesn't hover 20,000 feet above his subject and just give you an overview—instead, you are right there on the ground level. He has a rare ability to get people to tell him things that they wouldn't tell other people, maybe not even themselves. He earns their trust by hanging around, by not pushing or manipulating. By being genuinely interested.

"Because Sager doesn't put any barriers between us and his characters, and because he renders them so thoughtfully and with such compassion, readers are allowed to focus on the drama of the stories. Above all, Sager doesn't get in the way of the story. He is not a commentator or a pundit. He doesn't analyze, his pieces don't have an obvious aim or thesis. His prose is so direct and unfussy, it's almost invisible, like a camera. And yet there is a propulsion to it because in almost every sentence you'll find a fact—that blessed newspaper training again. The sentences flow with a definite rhythm, but Sager's style is unadorned with falsity, unburdened by over-interpretation. He's a natural story-teller. You never get the feeling he's there just to show off, only to entertain you."

—Alex Belth, editor of EsquireClassic.com and
The Stacks Reader Series

ALSO BY MIKE SAGER

Non Fiction

Scary Monsters and Super Freaks:
Stories of Sex, Drugs, Rock 'n' Roll, and Murder

Revenge of the Donut Boys:
True Stories of Lust, Fame, Survival, and Multiple Personality

The Someone You're Not:
True Stories of Sports, Celebrity, Politics & Pornography

Stoned Again: The High Times and
Strange Life of a Drugs Correspondent

Vetville: True Stories of the U.S. Marines at War and at Home

The Devil and John Holmes - 25th Anniversary Author's Edition: And
Other True Stories of Drugs, Porn and Murder

Janet's World: The Inside Story of Washington Post
Pulitzer Fabulist Janet Cooke

Travels with Bassem:
A Palestinian and a Jew Find Friendship in a War-Torn Land

The Lonely Hedonist:
True Stories of Sex, Drugs, Dinosaurs and Peter Dinklage

Tattoos & Tequila: To Hell and Back with One of Rock's
Most Notorious Frontmen

Shaman: The Mysterious Life and Impeccable
Death of Carlos Castaneda

Hunting Marlon Brando: A True Story

Fiction

Deviant Behavior, A Novel

High Tolerance, A Novel

THE DEVIL &
JOHN HOLMES
and Other True Stories of
Drugs, Porn and Murder

25th Anniversary Author's Edition

MIKE SAGER

THE DEVIL &
JOHN HOLMES

and Other True Stories of Drugs, Porn and Murder

25th Anniversary Author's Edition

MIKE SAGER

"You hold your controversial subjects up to the viewer like a diamond, let light shine through all their different facets, and just show us what's there without placing blame or judgement. You write kindly and fairly. And truthfully. I fell asleep with a smile on my face after reading what you wrote about our time together, which was very nice—I was afraid to read it because people want to write scandalous and hurtful things about porn-stars, but you didn't. Thank you."
                    —Asia Carrera, writing about "The Porn Identity"

TABLE OF CONTENTS

John Holmes was a porn star. Eddie Nash was a drug lord. Their association ended in one of the most brutal mass murders in the history of Los Angeles. First published in *Rolling Stone* in June, 1989, the story inspired the classic movies *Boogie Nights*, with Mark Wahlberg, and *Wonderland* with Val Kilmer. The author's version with restored cuts and updates added on the thirty-second anniversary of publication.

Bonus Features:
More True Stories of Drugs, Porn and Murder

Savannah was a gorgeous porn starlet, among the first of the luminescent Vivid Girls, with a taste for handsome rock stars, fast cars, expensive designer gowns... and copious amounts of drugs to quiet her demons. When things fell apart, she could see only one way out.

Swingers like to say that when you enter the door of the orgy room, you leave your clothes and your labels behind you. Welcome to the Elite International Couples' Fantasy weekend in Pensacola, Florida, where anyone can be a swan.

When his wife decamps from the household, leaving his life and his bank account in tatters, our hero takes a much-needed assignment traveling the country in search of... retired porn starlets. From Nina Hartley's toy-filled dungeon, to Kay Taylor Parker's spirit-filled studio, to Asia Carrera's split-level hideaway in the mountains north of Las Vegas: How one man gets his mojo back.

FOREWORD

Let's be clear: Sager couldn't have screwed this up if he tried. "The Devil and John Holmes" has everything you could want in a magazine story: Sex, drugs, murder. A fourteen-inch penis. It had to be great. There was no other way.

But here's the secret. For all the freebasing and the blood, the satin bikini briefs and decorative human skulls, the porn and the binges and the deathbed confessions, "The Devil and John Holmes" is a love story. At least it is in Sager's hands.

I interviewed Mike last winter for our podcast. The plan was to discuss his greatest hits and I expected to spend much of the time talking about "Holmes"; I was desperate to hear the director's cut you're about to read. Before we sat down, I even asked him to make sure I eventually moved onto other questions for fear that I'd spend the whole time talking about the story, a favorite of mine since I'd first read it a decade before in Mike's *Scary Monsters and Super Freaks* collection.

We never got there.

Instead of dissecting his stories, Mike preached the gospel of listening. For two hours, in a sweaty room with my dog baking under the table, he made the case for why a good reporter must first be a good person. We talked about empathy and fear and insecurity and using every last bit of yourself to see things from someone else's point of view. About love, really.

John Holmes was a shithead for much of his life. He got people killed, beat women, stole, lied, cheated. Tough guy to love. And yet there were two women who did just that, each in her own way, and each to her own great detriment. Sharon Holmes saw her husband as a desperate, lonely kid who needed a mom. Dawn Schiller, who was drawn into Holmes' world at just 15, saw him first as a god and later as the Devil.

Mike was the first reporter ever to interview Sharon and Dawn. He didn't need to. Without a word from either of them, the tale you're about to read would still be a thriller. The most prolific male porn star of all time gets caught up in a gruesome murder, set against the drug-fueled hedonism of 1970s Los Angeles. It's magazine gold.

But for Sager, that wasn't enough. There were people who loved John Holmes, that shithead, and he had to know why.

Max Linsky is a founding editor
of Longform.org

AUTHOR'S INTRODUCTION

The Devil and John Holmes" was my eighth story for *Rolling Stone*, my second as a contract writer. It was 1989. I was thirty-two years old. The magazine called us contributing editors; I could hardly believe I was included every other week on the same masthead with the likes of Hunter S. Thompson, Susan Orlean, P.J. O'Rourke, Peter Travers, and Kurt Loder.

Rolling Stone in those days was just like you'd imagine. The walls were hung with Holy Grail stuff like the Annie Leibovitz photograph of a naked John Lennon draped around Yoko. The first *Rolling Stone* editor I ever met, David Rosenthal, kept a big colorful bird in a cage on his windowsill, which overlooked Central Park. The first editor I ever worked with was Carolyn White, married to Pulitzer Prize winner—and personal hero—Richard Ben Cramer. The staff was peopled with hip geniuses who wore interesting clothes; traipsing through was the occasional visiting rock star or politician. You could buy cocaine downstairs in the production department —mixed with the ink smell and sour nicotine haze was the skunky aroma of green sensimilla.

My direct boss at *Rolling Stone* was Robert Love. It seemed like the perfect name for the job. He was a native New Yorker, an Irishman with a streak of sadness in his blue-gray eyes. His tortoise shell glasses made him look like a young professor, a forelock falling over one lens. Love would eventually serve a long stint as managing editor of *Rolling Stone*, the chief man under editor and publisher Jann Wenner.

As my editor, Love assigned me stories, edited my copy, audited my expenses, taught me about using full stops between scenes instead of transitions, and generally nurtured me and my fledgling career as a national magazine writer. Over the years, I would come to care for him as both a friend and father figure.

To me, editors have always felt like parents—people who enable you, people with whom you clash, people who you try above all else to make proud. It's a classic co-dependent deal, because even though writers need editors for the work, even though much of the process of becoming a writer has to do with chasing these people down in hopes of serving them, the fact is, editors need writers to produce the work that distinguishes them—in the end, an editor is only as good as the work he or she is able to pull out of others.

Love and I spent a lot of time together at work and at play, much of it in the office (a guitar in the corner; a bottle of scotch in the drawer). The well-known literary watering hole, Elaine's, was another haunt; our go-to dealer, codenamed Father Dave, lived in the east nineties, conveniently up the street. I'm pretty sure Love danced at my wedding in Washington, D.C., though things from that night, and many others during the period, remain a little hazy. I do remember for sure that no matter what we did, we had a great time and a deep bond. Working with Love, I felt understood as a writer, one of the greatest gifts we sort can enjoy.

As it happened, Love also edited Hunter S. Thompson. As a frequent overnight guest at Love's apartment, on the Upper West Side, I would sometimes be present when Love edited the great man. Thompson's process happened mostly at night. As the hours passed, Love scissored and taped and retyped and willed together the somewhat disjointed dispatches that were spewing out of his fax machine, some of it scrawled, some of it typed, some of it carefully cajoled and prospected from the dark and drug-addled recesses of Thompson's brilliant mind by his assistant of the moment.

A few years later, when Thompson was arrested on drug and sexual assault charges, I was dispatched by *Rolling Stone* to Woody Creek to "cover" Thompson's case—and to lend to the entire grandiose affair an on-the-ground presence by the home office. (I still remember the antiquated language of the fax, on *Rolling Stone* letterhead, sent by Wenner in advance of me, a copy of which I carried in my leather backpack like a letter of intro-duction: "We're sending our man Sager. He's one of our best. He will be at your service.") Thompson's woes stemmed from a visit to his compound in 1990 by a former porn director, who would later describe cocaine use to authorities and accuse Thompson of giving her a tittie twister when she refused to join him in his hot tub. An 11-hour search of Thompson's house turned up small quantities of various drugs and a few sticks of dynamite.

Upon arrival at Owl Farm, I discovered that Thompson's usual cast of trusted functionaries and hangers-on, spooked by the unforgiving legal spotlight and Thompson's own distraught and often erratic state of mind—not to mention his fondness for knives, firearms, and explosives—had run for the hills.

There seemed only one course of action: I volunteered to be Thompson's man Friday.

Entering Thompson's gonzo world was a little like falling through the looking glass. Everything was faster, louder, more dramatic, hyper-real. It was as if Thompson's head was encased in a giant fishbowl filled with smoke. Some of the stuff that was happening in real time managed to penetrate. Other stuff, not so much. He had this way of twisting and building on what he perceived was happening until whole new worlds were forged. That's what we all loved about his writing. In person, it was like living with Don Quixote.

And so it was that I became his faithful Sancho Panza. I did his bidding around the house, heating salmon croquets for lunch, bandaging his fingers when he cut them sharpening his knives, throwing bloody clothing into the washer, lighting enor-mous fires in the stone fireplace as the sun set—he insisted on dousing the logs with gasoline to enliven the show; at one point I jumped back and cut my bald head on a rusty nail; now I was bleeding too. I was given an old manual typewriter to take back with me to my not-at-all modest digs at a hotel in Aspen, where I worked into the wee hours polishing the rough columns the master was writing for a newspaper in San Francisco. "Gotta keep the cash stream flowing," he mumbled insistently.

My days would begin in the late morning, around eleven, with an edgy trip up Thompson's walkway; his watch-peacocks screeched like tortured ghouls from high in the bare trees. As it turned out, my initial duty of every shift was to receive from Thompson a baggie full of cocaine, usually about a quarter of an ounce, seven grams. The coke back then, if you got the unadulterated stuff, was more rocky and crystalline. It could even have a pinkish hue. You couldn't snort it as it was. You had to render it into powder, usually with a fresh, single-edged razor blade. For greater efficiency, Thompson deployed a device that I remember being called a Deering Blender. Constructed of Tiffany-colored blue plastic, as big around as the base of a coffee mug, with a crank on the top, the Deering resembled a finer version of the multi-chambered marijuana grinders commonly in use today. When I was done cranking, a small glittery snowdrift was left gathered on the mirror.

Thompson liked to remove the ink cartridge from one of those old-school Bic pens. There were ink cartridges littered everywhere around the house; often they'd come into contact with one of his multiple burning cigarettes and melt and leak. He'd use the clear chamber of the Bic as a straw. With his fingertip securing the tiny hole, he'd dip into the pile and snort heroically… and off we'd go, into the day and its many adventures, which lasted, on average, about thirty-six hours. One such period concluded in the wee hours with a pistol shot into the ceiling. Another came with the confession that he was lonely and wanted some privacy to call someone. "Hey cool," I said with jocular empathy. "Sometimes a man needs to get laid." Thompson looked at me soberly. "Sometimes a man just needs a hug."

We were together for nearly three weeks; I wrote two stories about the case before it was dismissed after a pre-trial. Lord help me, my first draft of the first story was written in coke-fueled, rainbow-colored, faux-Thompson prose. Thankfully, a verbal face slap was properly issued by my able then-editor, Robert Vare.

With Thompson I felt a little like Ebenezer Scrooge visiting with the Ghost of Christmas Future. Important lessons were learned, the first of which was not to mix hard drugs and alcohol with the practice of writing. The second lesson was a little more subtle. In creating a voice for yourself as a writer, I think it's important to make sure that the real you isn't swept away. In the years before his death, Thompson and I would have two more adventures together in New York, one at four in the morning involving publishing honcho David Hirshey, a lost ball of hashish, and the Pope of Pot, who owned one of the pioneering marijuana services in New York.

Notwithstanding all the stagecraft and showboating and real and perceived drug craziness, Hunter Thompson was a sweet man with a large but damaged heart. For much of his life, I'm pretty sure, he was lonely in a crowd of merry makers. It's good to know he spent his last years with someone who truly loved him and meant him well. It may be a measure of his mental state that he took his own life with his son and grandson in the house. He will always be a part of me, one of my heroes.

As an editor and a friend, Bob Love's greatest gift to me was wonderful assignments. "A Boy and His Dog in Hell" was about kids fighting pit bulldogs in the ravaged ghettos of North Philadelphia. "Inhuman Bondage," was about a raid on a USDA research facility outside Washington, D.C. with citizen-guerillas from the Animal Liberation Front. When Love assigned me "The Death of a High School Narc," about a murder in a small Texas town during the early stirrings of the drug war, he did so thinking I was ready to do my first, big, true crime re-creation; he guided me through the difficult process as only a nurturer of his caliber could. "The Devil and John Holmes" was only my second attempt at true crime reportage. Like the subject himself, the task seemed gargantuan.

As it happened, the Holmes story was hatched one day in the fall of 1988. I was in New York, up from my home in

Washington, DC, visiting the *Rolling Stone* offices. It was a good time for a writer to be seen in headquarters; my last piece for the magazine was on the newsstands—an account of my summer living with a Mexican-American gang in Venice, California during the early days of the crack epidemic. I was sitting on a desk top visiting with one of the cute assistants when I spied Jann Wenner making a bee-line toward me—at that point, we'd not yet met.

Wenner is a small man like myself; his hair was wavy and full, shiny with whatever slickum men were using during that era of Pat Riley's Showtime Lakers and Michael Douglas' Gordon Gekko. He was the kind of man whose attention you wanted badly but learned to kind of regret.

Two sentences into our very first conversation, without provocation, Wenner dropped suddenly to all fours, acting out a part in my article where the Venice homeboys are feeling around on the floor for little pieces of crack that may have fallen, a behavior well known to many during those coke-tweaked times. With this millionaire publisher down on his hands and knees in front of me—this towering historic figure who had helped define the notion of youth culture and founded the Rock and Roll Hall of Fame, a man who had already played himself in several movies, crawling around on the chic gray industrial carpet of this 23rd floor office in this ornate deco building in the Big Apple, just across from FAO Schwartz and the Plaza Hotel—I couldn't help but notice one little detail: The lapels of his beautiful, bespoke blue wool pinstripe suit were dusted with tell-tale white flakes.

A little later that day, I was recounting my experience to Love in his office when he pulled out a news clipping about the AIDS death of the seminal porn star John Holmes, who'd been involved in the bludgeoning murders of four Hollywood lowlifes known as the Wonderland Gang. Holmes had earlier in the decade been tried and acquitted of the bloody crime, which would become known in the press as the Four on the Floor Murders. With Holmes' death the case had been reopened by the

Los Angeles County District Attorney's Office. Indicted in the murders were a Palestinian coke dealer and night club impresario—Adel Nasrallah, a.k.a. Eddie Nash—and his large, blubbery bodyguard, Gregory Diles.

It was a story unlike any other I'd yet done or even attempted, with three distinct reporting wars to wage—a lot of territory to claim. There was the human story of a man with a reputed fourteen-inch penis. There was the story of the porn industry that Holmes helped define—and bring into the living rooms and bedrooms of ordinary people. And there was the murder story—a tale of the wild, pre-twelve-step days in LaLa Land, when a gram of coke and a couple of Valiums were *de rigueur* as a pocket accessory. I was scared, excited, and overwhelmed. To pull this off, it would take every skill I'd yet learned as a journalist and then some.

Out of fear, afraid to fail on this big stage I'd talked myself onto, I assembled and contacted a twenty-page list of sources. I found the records room four stories beneath the courthouse that held all the files and evidence from the earlier court case (somebody later stole it); I found an employee who didn't mind helping me sort things out and make copies. I interviewed porn stars, cops, federal prisoners, druggies, lawyers, film critics, and porn entrepreneurs. I took a lot of collect calls from prisons. All these bits and pieces and recollections and quotes were gathered into what I like to call my "bowl of details," the bits of raw material that became this story.

Somewhere along in the reporting process, I heard that Holmes, before he'd become a porn star, had married a young nurse and lived a square and ordinary life in the suburbs. Searching for her, I'd somehow come across a man who claimed to have the exclusive rights to the woman's story. At the beginning of the negotiations, he asked for money, creative input, and even a shared byline. I still have the file with all the back and forth. As I recall, I ended up going around the guy—I finally made the connection through a *Los Angeles Times* reporter named Rob Stewart. Reporters don't always share contacts, but Stewart is a cool guy and agreed to forward my info to the former wife of John C. Holmes.

To keep expenses down while reporting the piece, I'd stayed in a little suite (where I could cook my own meals) at a rundown hotel on Wilshire Boulevard owned by a nice family of South Asians. I remember the knock on my door, the strong smell of curry in hallways.

At long last, Sharon Holmes stood in front of me.

And she'd arrived with a younger friend—which was weird. But at this point, after working so long on this piece, and hearing everything I'd heard, well, nothing was weird, if you know what I mean.

As the interview began, I learned the other woman's name was Dawn Schiller. For the purposes of the story, she wanted to be known as Jeana.

Starting at the age of fifteen, she'd been John Holmes' mistress.

And here was the really interesting thing: They were friends now. More than friends. Sharon had become the mother to Dawn she'd never had.

For the next twelve hours, Sharon and Dawn sat at the little round Formica dinette table in my room and regaled me with the incredibly intimate details that helped me portray the human side of this larger-than-life figure. The stories they told were unimaginable. They helped me turn a rather one-dimensional tale of a man with a mythological penis into the story of a real man, the kind of guy who'd use his self-taught skill as a carpenter to turn his suburban bathroom into a faux outhouse, complete with a half-moon in the door. As the two women spoke, it was everything I could do to keep from jumping up and down.

After a number of follow up phone interviews with both women and with other sources they suggested, and after a lot of writing, editing, fact-checking, and lawyering, "The Devil and John Holmes" ran in the issue of *Rolling Stone* dated June 15, 1989. Paul McCartney was featured on the cover; the story was even given a coveted cover line. Because of the space limitations of paper publishing, the piece ran at twelve thousand words. The "author's refurbishment" contained in this twenty-fifth anniversary edition weighs in at just under twenty thousand words. It was a pleasure to go back through and be able to restore so much astounding stuff to its rightful place in the manuscript, and also to smooth out some spots where saving details took precedence over literary voice. I remember working late into the night with copy chief Alice Gabriel to eliminate widows at the end of paragraphs by trimming sentences, allowing me to restore additional information. I will always be grateful that someone would follow me down such a rabbit hole in the interest of saving little factoids, each one so beautiful and hard won, as any investigator knows.

Since the piece was published, a number of Hollywood types have optioned "The Devil and John Holmes" for film, including the actor Eric Roberts (who wanted to direct; his homage to Bob Fosse's *Star 80*), and the screenwriter who wrote *Bill and Ted's Excellent Adventure II*. I am also blessed and cursed by the fact that two popular movies which were inspired and partially based on my story, *Boogie Nights* and *Wonderland*, did not credit me or include me as a financial participant—though I was pleased the *Wonderland* producers did compensate Sharon Holmes and Dawn Schiller for the use of their life stories.

The truth of the matter is that I did *not* own the rights to Holmes' story or to the life stories of any of the characters in this piece, so nothing is owed to me that I can tell. The way I see it, I was lucky to have such a great story placed in my lap by a great editor at a great magazine—though I have always been left to wonder if the story is popular because I did a good job or because it's about a guy with a reputed fourteen-inch penis.

In fact, it was not fourteen-inches.

The exact dimensions are reported faithfully within.

—Mike Sager
La Jolla, California

THE DEVIL AND JOHN HOLMES

John Holmes was a porn star. Eddie Nash was a drug lord. Their association ended in one of the most brutal mass murders in the history of Los Angeles. First published in *Rolling Stone* in June, 1989, the story inspired the classic movies *Boogie Nights,* with Mark Wahlberg, and *Wonderland* with Val Kilmer. The author's version with restored cuts and updates added on the thirty-second anniversary of publication.

Deep in Laurel Canyon, the Wonderland Gang was planning its last heist. It was Sunday evening and the drugs were gone, the money was gone, the situation was desperate. They'd sold a pound of baking soda for a quarter of a million dollars: there were contracts out on their lives. Now they had another idea. They sat around a glass table in the breakfast nook. Before them were two pairs of handcuffs, a stolen police badge, several automatic pistols, and a dog-eared sheet of paper—a floor plan. They needed a score. This was it.

There were seven of them meeting in the house on Wonderland Avenue, a jaundiced stucco box on a steep, winding road in the hills above Hollywood. Joy Audrey Miller, forty-six, held the lease. She was thin, blonde, foul-mouthed, a heroin addict with seven arrests. She had two daughters, had once been married to a Beverly Hills attorney. A year ago, she'd been busted for dealing drugs out of the Wonderland house. Six months ago she'd had a double mastectomy. Her lover was Billy DeVerell, forty-two. He was also a heroin addict. He had a slight build, a pockmarked face, a record of thirteen arrests. He favored cowboy boots and dirty jeans. "He looked like a guy you might find in a dive bar in El Paso," according to a neighbor.

Sharing the house with Miller and DeVerell was Ronald Launius, thirty-seven. Blond and bearded, Launius claimed to have been a sergeant in the Air Force. He'd served federal time for drug smuggling. A California cop called him "one of the coldest people I ever met." According to police records, Launius had been arrested in connection with the 1973 death of an informant. Charges were dropped after a witness was killed in a shootout.

The house at 8763 Wonderland Avenue rented for $750 a month. There was a garage on the first floor; the second and third floors had balconies facing the street. A stairway, leading from the garage to the front door, was caged in iron bars. There was a telephone at the entrance, an electronic deadbolt on the gate, two pit bulls sleeping on the steps.

Though elaborately secure, the house was paint-cracked and rust-stained, an eyesore in a trendy neighborhood. Laurel Canyon had long been a prestige address, an earthy, woodsy setting just minutes from Sunset Boulevard and all the glitter and rush of Tinseltown. Tom Mix and Harry Houdini once lived there among the quail and scrub pine and coyotes. Later, in the sixties, the canyon attracted writers, artists, rock stars, actors, plenty of trust-funders, and a large community of drug dealers who kept all the various fires stoked. Number 8763 Wonderland Avenue had some history of its own: Paul Revere and the Raiders, a Beatles-era band, had once lived there.

By the eighties, California governor Jerry Brown was living on Wonderland Avenue, and Steven Spielberg was building on a lot nearby. The house at 8763 had passed from a raucous group of women—neighbors recall naked women being tossed from the first-floor balcony—to the members of the Wonderland Gang. Things at the house were always hopping; someone was always showing up with a scam. Miller, DeVerell, and Launius needed drugs every day. They were always looking for an opportunity. Jewelry stores, convenience stores, private homes, a pet shop owner with an antique coin collection, a crooked cop with three kilos of marijuana in the trunk of his car. They would try anything, as long as it meant money or drugs.

"You could always tell when they had some drugs to sell," recalls the neighbor across the street. "There was a lot of traffic, all day, all night," says another neighbor. "Everything from Volkswagens to a Rolls-Royce Silver Shadow. Like thirty to forty cars over a two or three-day period. They would throw brown bags of dope off the balcony to the people in the cars. Sometimes people would park and stay a couple of hours, or sometimes they left quickly. There was shouting, laughing, and loud rock 'n' roll music twenty-four hours a day."

At the moment, on this evening of June 28, 1981, Wonderland Avenue was quiet. Five men and two women were meeting in the breakfast nook, sitting in swivel chairs, leaning against walls. The floor plan before them showed a three-bedroom, high-end tract house on a cul-de-sac in the San Fernando Valley. It had a pool and a sunken living room, a white stone façade, a chain-link fence surrounding the perimeter. Inside were smoked mirrors and a rare, theater-sized TV. Ready for the taking was a painting by Rembrandt, a jade and ivory collection, sterling silver, jewelry, a number of firearms and, most appealing of all, large quantities of money and drugs.

The man who owned the house was named Adel Nasrallah. He was known as Eddie Nash. A naturalized American, Nash came to California from Palestine in the early fifties. In 1960 he opened a hot-dog stand on Hollywood Boulevard. He cooked, served, and waited tables all by himself. By the midseventies, Nash held thirty-six liquor licenses, owned real estate and other assets worth more than $30 million.

Nash had clubs of all kinds; he catered to all predilections. The Kit Kat was a strip club. The Seven Seas was a bus-stop joint across Hollywood Boulevard from Mann's Chinese Theaters. It had a tropical motif, a menu of special drinks, a Polynesian revue, sometimes belly dancers. His gay clubs were the first in LA to allow same-sex dancing. His black club was like a Hollywood Harlem, jazz and pinkie rings and wide-brimmed straw hats. The Starwood, on Santa Monica Boulevard, featured cutting-edge rock 'n' roll. In the late seventies, Los Angeles police averaged twenty-five drug busts a month at the Starwood. One search of the premises yielded a cardboard box containing four thousand counterfeit Quaaludes. A sign on the box, written in blue Magic Marker, said, FOR DISTRIBUTION AT BOX OFFICE.

Nash was a drug dealer and a heavy user. His drug of choice was freebase, home-cooked crack cocaine, and he was smoking it at the rate of two to three ounces a day. He always had large quantities of coke, heroin, Quaaludes and other drugs at the house. His bodyguard, Gregory DeWitt Diles, was a karate expert and convicted felon who weighed a blubbery 300 pounds. According to an eyewitness, Diles once chased a man out of the Kit Kat and emptied his .38 revolver into the man's car. The car was on the other side of Santa Monica Boulevard, across six lanes of traffic. The time was 2:30 in the afternoon. No one was injured.

Nash and Diles were well known on Sunset Strip. "Eddie Nash assumed he deserved a certain amount of respect," says one denizen. "He treated people right. Nobody who ever worked for him didn't make good money. And he always stood up. If somebody needed to get out of jail, if somebody needed whatever, you could go explain the problem to him. If it was a decent problem—not just 'I need money for dope,' but really a problem—Eddie was in his pocket right now. No problem, no questions asked. But one thing's for sure. If somebody fucked with Eddie Nash, they got dead."

Now, in the breakfast nook, in one of the swivel chairs, a tall, gaunt man with curly hair and a sparse beard pointed to the floor plan he had sketched.

"Here, this back bedroom, that's Diles' room," he said. "He keeps a sawed-off shotgun under the blanket... Here, this is Nash's room. There's a floor safe in the closet, right... over... here," he indicated. "There's a black attaché case somewhere in there, and also this metal strong box. And don't forget, on the dresser, there's a big vial of heroin."

"You sure about this, donkey dick?" asked Tracy McCourt, the gang's wheelman.

"Fuck you, dirt bag," said John Holmes, thirty-six.

"Fuck you, Holmes!" shot back DeVerall from across the table. "You owe us. You owe *me*! You better be right about this shit."

"Hey, it's cool," Holmes said. He flashed his well-known smirk, always the man with the plan. "I know Eddie. He loves me. He thinks I'm *famous*."

John Holmes was famous, at least in some circles. What he was famous for was his penis.

In a career that would span twenty years, Holmes told people he'd made 2,274 hard-core pornographic films and had sex with fourteen thousand women. At the height of his popularity he earned three thousand dollars a day on films and almost as much turning tricks, servicing wealthy men and women on both coasts and in Europe, according to a Los Angeles vice detective who used Holmes as an informant on prostitution and porn cases for fifteen years.

Since the late sixties, Holmes had traded on his natural endowment. According to legend, his penis, when erect, measured between eleven and fifteen inches in length. Recently, however, Holmes biggest commodity had been trouble. He was freebasing one hit of coke every ten to fifteen minutes, swallowing forty to fifty Valium a day to cut the edge. The drugs affected his penis; he couldn't get it up, he couldn't work in porn. Now he'd been reduced to being a drug delivery boy for the Wonderland Gang. His mistress, Dawn, who'd been with him since she was fifteen, was turning tricks to support his habit. They were living out of the trunk of his estranged wife's Chevy Malibu. Holmes was stealing luggage off conveyers at LA International, buying appliances with his wife's credit cards and fencing them for cash. (In fact Eddie Nash had a microwave behind the bar at his house that Holmes had traded for drugs.) Holmes was into Nash for a small fortune. And now Holmes owed the Wonderland Gang, too. He'd messed up a delivery, had a big argument with DeVerell and Launius; they took back his

JOHN C. HOLMES

SUPERSTAR

ALL NEW
ALL ORIGINAL

Starring **JOHN C. HOLMES** • **LAURIEN DOMINIQUE**

Amber Hunt • Paul Thomas

David Blair • Laura Bourbon

Directed by Alan B. Colberg

Original Music Score
Robert Sommer
Title Song Available
Mystic Records

PACIFIC COAST FILMS

RATED
X
IN COLOR

AN IN-DEPTH INTERVIEW

key to Wonderland and Launius punched him out. "You need to make this right," the gang told him. Holmes' addled synapses played him a picture: Eddie Nash.

"So you go in," Launius was saying to Holmes, reviewing the plan. "You talk to Nash, whatever, you tell him you got to take a piss. Then what?"

"I leave the sliding door unlocked. This one," said Holmes, pointing to the floor plan. "Here in the back. The guest bedroom. Then I leave. I come back to Wonderland. Tell you it's all clear. Then you guys go over with the badge and handcuffs, act like it's a bust, and clean them out."

"Why the fuck don't we just kill 'em?" asked McCourt. "Let's go in there, get what we need, and kill everybody. That way we don't leave no witnesses."

"No way," Holmes insisted. "No one gets hurt. Nash is connected. We don't want *that*."

And so the plan was fixed. At midnight, the Wonderland people scraped together $400, and Holmes, whose pretense for entrance would be buying drugs, drove off to Nash's house.

It was 1.6 miles from Wonderland Avenue to Nash's house on Dona Lola Place, which was fortuitous because the stolen Ford Granada driven by the Wonderland Gang was running on empty. In the car were DeVerell, Launius, McCourt, and a man named David Lind, a friend of Launius'. Lind and his girlfriend had come down three weeks earlier from Sacramento to stay at Wonderland. An ex-convict who'd served time for burglary, forgery, and assault to commit rape, Lind had been invited to town, he would later tell a court, to practice his "profession," committing crimes. "I was in town because I thought Launius was a very treacherous individual... I liked his attitude," he told the court.

Feeling bitter about the fact that Lind confiscated his .45—*who goes to a goddam home invasion without a piece?* he asked himself—McCourt drove up the hill on Laurel Canyon Boulevard... across Mulholland Drive... over the crest of the Santa Monica Mountains... down into the Valley. It was

8:30 on a Monday morning. The sun was warm and diffuse. Sprinklers were ticking water across lawns. Rush hour was on. Though Holmes had left Wonderland at midnight, he had stayed at Eddie Nash's for six hours, smoking up the $400 he'd taken to spend, helping himself to a little more of Nash's largess. Nash was extremely hospitable. He always called Holmes "my brother." It was part Arab affectation, part drug-fueled affectation, part genuine familiarity. They'd known each other for three years, a long time to have the same drug connection. A relationship had blossomed. Eddie got the charge of knowing and serving this famous porn star; Holmes got the star treatment and plenty of extra drugs.

As night stretched into morning, Holmes had an attack of conscience, a glimmer of an understanding that knocking over Eddie Nash might lead to a lot of trouble. Nash knew the Wonderland people. He'd never met them, but he had, through Holmes, given them a thousand dollar loan. Nash held several stolen antique guns as collateral. Holmes muttered something to Nash about the gang. "The Wonderland People," he said, his jaw locked in the rictus of a freebase run. "They have guns. They want to hold you…" But Nash had been on a ten-day drug binge, testimony would later indicate. He had hardly slept. Whatever Holmes was mumbling, Nash wasn't getting the gist. As they continued to smoke, as Holme's' supply of coke dwindled— disappearing before his eyes in the tricky way a stash does, flush one moment, crumbs the next—his conscience was overruled by his jones. He excused himself, left the room, and unlocked the sliding door as planned.

Holmes arrived back at Wonderland just after dawn, announced the coast clear. "The time is right," he told Lind portentously.

Only there was one hitch.

DeVerell, Launius, and McCourt were all heroin addicts.

All of them were nodded out.

Two and a half hours later, the Wonderland Gang was finally awake, fixed and ready to do some crime. "It was like tryin' to wake the dead," McCourt would later joke by telephone from a prison in a southeastern state. Changing the plan on the fly, it was decided that Holmes should drive to Nash's house once again to make sure the sliding door was still open. This time, the gang decided not to wait for his return.

They met the porn star at the corner of Laurel Canyon Boulevard and Dona Lola, Holmes driving back toward them. Both cars slowed, pulled even in the middle of the street. Holmes rolled down his window, McCourt rolled down his.

"It's *time*," Holmes said portentously, and then he smiled and raised his fist. "Get 'em boys!"

John Curtis Holmes had the longest, most prolific career in the history of pornography. He had sex on-screen with two generations of leading ladies, from Seka and Marilyn Chambers to Traci Lords, Ginger Lynn, and Italian Member of Parliament Ciccolina. The first man to win the X-Rated Critics Organization Best Actor Award, Holmes was an idol and an icon, the most visible male porn star of his time.

Holmes started in the business around 1968. He began with nude dancing and photo layouts, went on to "loops." Loops were the first porn movies to be made available to large numbers of viewers, short, black-and-white films that were viewed in adult bookstores. There was a booth, a curtain. Quarters were pumped into a slot. The screen was not much larger than an iPhone's. By some accounts, Holmes made more than a thousand of these eight-millimeter loops, and also a great number of longer "stag" films. Stags had no plot. The women were not goddesses. They had a lot of hair down there. The men were not very god-like, either. Often they kept their black socks on while performing. To watch a stag you needed to rent a film projector. Most commonly, you'd see one at a frat house, a bachelor party, or VWF hall.

When Holmes entered the field, the sexual revolution was changing the cultural landscape. The sixties, the pill, "free love," communes, wife swapping, the perverse creativity of mixed-media artists who were pushing the limit, trying to shock—all of these things created an atmosphere in which porn could blossom. The pivotal event in porn history was the public release of *Deep Throat*, starring Linda Lovelace and Harry Reems, in 1972. Though the movie, when it began to appear at theaters around the country, was branded as obscene and was closed down almost everywhere it played, its producers contested the charges in the courts and eventually won. In the end, *Deep Throat* was massively consumed by an enthusiastic public. With the release the same year of *The Devil in Miss Jones* and *Behind the Green Door*, porn became part of popular culture. Suddenly, Johnny Carson was telling *Deep Throat* jokes on The Tonight Show. (The name was further iconized when journalism's famous investigative team, Bob Woodward and Carl Bernstein, chose Deep Throat as the code name for their source of insider information on the Watergate break-in and the involvement of then-president Richard M. Nixon.)

One day in 1970, Holmes met Hawaiian producer Bob Chinn. He showed Chinn his portfolio of stills, then stripped. Inspired, Chinn sat down that evening and wrote a three-page screenplay. A partnership was born. This would lead, in the midseventies, to Holmes' most successful role, as Johnny Wadd, hard-boiled detective. It was porn's parody of Sam Spade, who'd been portrayed most notably by the film actor Humphrey Bogart.

Holmes' Johnny Wadd, wrote porn gadfly and historian Al Goldstein in *Screw* magazine, was "a thin, bony, trench-coated shamus, outrageously horny, bedding down with client and quarry alike." In Goldstein's opinion, "it was a goofy, crudely made series," but it was wildly successful. In a way, Holmes was every man's gigolo, a polyester smoothy with a sparse mustache, a flying collar and lots of buttons undone. He wasn't threatening. He chewed gum and overacted. He took a lounge singer's approach to sex, deliberately gentle, ostentatiously artful, a homely guy with a pinkie ring and a big dick who was convinced he was every woman's dream. "That was one thing to be said of Holmes," Goldstein continued. "He was never the picture of the swaggering, violent male chauvinist. Quite the opposite: He was

John C. Holmes as Johnny Wadd
AS BIG AS ITS STARS!

The Greatest! The Boldest! The Best!

THE CHINA CAT

DAMON CHRISTIAN PRESENTS A BOB CHINN FILM

Copyright MCMLXXVII Freeway Film Corporation   All Rights Reserved

Starring **John C. Holmes** as Johnny Wadd
Also starring **Monti Stevens** • **Eileen Welles** • **Jenifer Richards**
With **Christian Sarver** • **John Seemen** • **Desiree Clearbranch**
Special Guest Star **Kyoto** as China Cat

ADULTS ONLY

Sound by Glen Glenn   Color by PFI   A Freeway Film Corporation Release quiet, gentle, almost artful when he fucked. He let his size do the posturing for him."

Holmes went on to make more than two thousand movies, titles such as *Teenage Cowgirls*, *Liquid Lips*, *China Cat*, and *Tapestry of Passion*. *Eruption*, a porn remake of *Double Indemnity*. *Dickman and Throbbin*, a lampoon of Batman and Robin. *Hard Candy* was a thriller shot in 3-D. *The Autobiography of a Flea*, a porn version of the famous book, was shot by the well-known Mitchell brothers, who reigned over a porn empire based in San Francisco. An X-rated but journalistically sound documentary of Holmes' life, made in 1981, was called *Exhausted*. It was fitting. John Holmes was everywhere.

In time, in porn circles Holmes became known as the King. Often he was likened to Errol Flynn, the great cinema swordsman of yesteryear. And like the leading men of yesteryear whose images were manufactured by the studios in order to give the public its thrills, most of what was known about Holmes was myth.

The way he told it to interviewers, Holmes was born in New York and lived with a rich aunt who'd been married fifteen times. The aunt sent him to fencing school, dancing school, a school of etiquette. They lived in London, Paris, Michigan, and Florida. He lost his virginity at the Florida house, when he was six, to his Swiss nanny, Frieda. The house was huge, with a gardener, cook, butler, and maid. Frieda took young John to the beach and gave him head, taught him how to give head. He had his first orgasm at eight, he said.

In high school, Holmes said, he slept with all but three of the girls in his class. He graduated from UCLA with majors, variously, in physical therapy, pediatric physical therapy, medicine, and political science. His first porn film was made while he was working his way through college. A girl from the dorm recommended him. The producer paid with a $100 check that bounced. Also while in college, he said, he danced "nude modern jazz ballet" and drove an ambulance. As a paramedic, he delivered

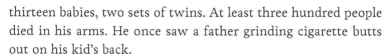

thirteen babies, two sets of twins. At least three hundred people died in his arms. He once saw a father grinding cigarette butts out on his kid's back.

When he became established as a porn star, Holmes said, he had a half dozen agents pulling in work for him. He made films nonstop, and he took eighty to ninety telephone calls a day from producers, distributors, actors, models, and fans. He had twenty-seven fan clubs; people wrote asking for locks of his pubic hair. (He liked to send poodle clippings, he said.) On movie sets, even though he was the star, he sometimes held boom mics and drove trucks, just to stay busy. He did all his own stunts—flying, sky diving, jumping from building to building, crashing motorcycles. He also liked to tinker with explosives. Once he blew an English double-decker bus into "about 90 million pieces" for a film. When he'd acted poorly in a movie, he felt bad for a month, felt like giving the director back his money.

Men, he said, asked Holmes to autograph their wives' breasts. Women asked him to deflower their daughters. One regular trick had him barge into her bedroom while she was watching TV, then tie her up and rape her. Her husband watched from the closet. Another regular trick of his, he said, was a high-priced hooker. Holmes was the only one who could *really* satisfy her; it took a professional of his caliber to make her come. Holmes said he received, by mail every month, between seventy-five and eighty written propositions for sex from women, and 200 from men. More than one thousand women had proposed marriage over the years, he said. He'd had sex in airplanes, helicopters, trains, elevators, kitchens, bathrooms. On rooftops, in caves, in storm cellars, in bomb shelters in Europe, under a table in a restaurant filled with people, fifty feet underwater while wearing scuba gear. He'd been with three governors, two of their wives, a congressman, a congressman's sister, a congressman's wife, and one senator, who was "really a freak."

Holmes said he owned ten different businesses. He was a gourmet cook. He had written twenty-nine books, including a how-to manual combining cooking and sex. He had six to eight different longtime girlfriends. He didn't believe in marriage. He collected gold pocket watches. As a rule, he never took any type of narcotic or dope, and no pills, not even aspirin or Rolaids. He didn't drink alcohol. The hardest thing he drank was coffee. That other stuff, he said, "is no good for you." When asked the dimensions of his famous organ, he liked to say it was "bigger than a pay phone, smaller than a Cadillac." When he was in a nasty mood, he said, he liked to dress right because his penis showed bigger on that side. He had to stop wearing underwear because he tore the elastic in too many pairs.

Holmes' voice was sly and ingratiating. He sounded a lot like Eddie Haskell on the old television show *Leave It to Beaver*; he actually bore some resemblance to the actor who played him. Above all, he said, he loved his work: "A happy gardener is one with dirty fingernails, and a happy cook is a fat cook. I never get tired of what I do because I'm a sex fiend. I'm very lusty."

"Ninety-nine times out of 100," he said another time, "a woman doesn't accept me for who I am. They don't accept me for my own sexuality. They see me as a fantasy. It's really hard to achieve what I want sexually and mentally from a relationship with somebody who's trying to fuck a Walt Disney character, which I'm not.

"When it comes to making love, I'm two different people. In my work life, I'm very professional with a personal touch. In my real life, I'm very personal with a professional touch. There's very little difference. I treat each woman like dirt. Ha, no. Just kidding. I treat them with respect and gentle kindness, whips and chains. Bondage, domination, and kisses."

John Curtis Holmes was born to Mary and Edward Holmes on August 8, 1944, in Pickaway County, Ohio, the youngest of three boys and a girl. Edward, a carpenter, was an alcoholic. Mary was a Bible-thumping Baptist. Holmes remembered screaming, yelling, his father puking all over the kids, all four of whom slept in the same bed. (Holmes got the outside because he had to go to

the bathroom most often. Often he'd end up on the floor.)

Holmes' parents separated when he was three, and Mary moved the family into a housing project in Columbus. They shared an apartment with another divorced woman and her two children. It was this woman who would become Holmes' first lover, when he was twelve and she was thirty-six. Many years later, when he first came to California as a young adult, Holmes stayed with the woman and her new husband. They were nudists. They introduced Holmes to the lifestyle.

When Holmes was eight, his mother married Harold, a manic-depressive who worked for the telephone company. They moved to a house on five acres in wooded, rural Pataskala, Ohio. Harold drank a lot. Once, he rammed his own hand into a harvesting machine. He lost his thumb and three fingers. At the hospital, as he came out of anesthesia, he said to Mary, "I'll never have to work again." He didn't. Mary went to work on an assembly line at a Western Electric plant.

Holmes was a shy and lonely kid who kept to himself and had perfect attendance at Sunday school. At home, Harold picked on Holmes. There were backhands, lectures, drunken rages. By the time Holmes' half-brother was born, Holmes was spending most of his time in the woods, hunting, trapping, fishing, staying away from Harold. Then one day Harold and Holmes had a big fight. Harold threw Holmes down the stairs into the basement and came after him. Holmes swung and knocked his stepfather out. On his sixteenth birthday, Holmes joined the Army. He served in the Signal Corps, spending three years in Nuremberg, Germany. He never went home again.

After mustering out of the Army at age nineteen, Holmes went to work as an ambulance driver, and soon thereafter he met Sharon Gebenini. Sharon was a nurse at USC County General, working on a team that was pioneering open-heart surgery. She was twenty, an Army brat. She and Holmes went to dinner, movies, concerts, parks, quiet places where they talked a lot. They were married in August 1965 at Fort Ord, California.

One summer day in 1968, Sharon came home a little early

Every Woman's
Dream

Every Man's
Fantasy

JOHN C. HOLMES IS THE

CALIFORNIA GIGOLO

STARRING JOHN C. HOLMES

Also Starring **VERI KNOTTY** • **KITTY SHAYNE**

And Introducing **VANESSA TIBBS**

A real-life debutante fulfilling her fantasy of starring in an XXX film.

With **LIZA DWYER** • **BARBARA BILLS** • **DON FERNANDO**

Special Guest Appearance by **KANDI BARBEAU**

Produced by **Elliot Lewis** • Music by **Jay Phillips** • Directed by **Bob Chinn**

xXx

IN COLOR

from work. Her new boss, a pediatrician, had shut down the office for the afternoon, and she'd gone to the market, planning a special dinner for her husband. He was skinny, she thought, and needed fattening up.

In those days Holmes was a string bean, six feet tall, 150 pounds, with his hair still cut in a military buzz. He had a thin little moustache that didn't quite meet in the middle. He always wore a white shirt, black trousers and black lace-up shoes. When Sharon and Holmes were first married, she says, he was very naïve, looking for the perfect relationship. He asked her to quit her job at County General and stay home. "He was a very dependent person. I was not. He was very possessive. He treated me like his exclusive material. He wouldn't even let me meet the people he worked with."

Recently Holmes had been drifting from job to job, trying to find a niche for himself. After quitting the ambulance service, he got work stirring vats of chocolate at a Coffee Nips factory in Glendale. He sold shoes, furniture, Fuller brushes door-to-door. He drove a forklift at a meatpacking plant in Cudahy until his lung collapsed from working in the freezer. Just recently, he had begun training to be a uniformed security guard. Sharon had gone back to work. They needed the money.

Unbeknownst to Sharon, following an encounter with a professional photographer named Joel in the bathroom of the poker parlor in Gardina he frequented, Holmes had recently started doing porn—still pictorials and dancing in clubs.

Now, home early from her job at a doctor's office, Sharon left her purse in the foyer, squeaked down the hall on white rubber soles to the bathroom of their one-bedroom apartment in Glendale. The door was open. Inside was her husband. He had a tape measure in one hand, his penis in the other.

"What are you doing?" she asked.

"What does it look like I'm doing?"

"Is there something wrong? Are you afraid it's withering and dying?" she said, laughing.

"No, I'm just curious," said Holmes.

Sharon went to the bedroom, lay down, read a magazine. Twenty minutes later, Holmes walked into the room. He had a full erection.

"It's incredible," said Holmes.

"What?"

"It goes from five inches all the way to ten. It's ten inches long, four inches around."

"That's great," said Sharon, turning a page of her magazine. "You want me to call the press?"

Her husband fixed her with a long stare. Finally he said, "I've got to tell you I've been doing something else, and I think I want to make it my life's work."

Holmes went on to say that he always wanted to be best in the world at something, and that he thought pornography just might be it. Sharon had been a virgin when they'd met. She was a good girl, a nurse. She wasn't very well versed on the darker sides of sex... or of life in general. Now her young husband was telling her he wanted to be a pornographer? "Can't you be arrested for doing that?"

"You can't be uptight about this," Holmes insisted, a refrain she would hear again and again for the next fifteen years. "This means absolutely nothing to me. It's like being a carpenter. These are my tools. I use them to make a living. When I come home at night, the tools stay on the job."

"Can't you see it from my point of view?" Sharon asked. "You are having sex with other women. It's like being married to a *hooker.*"

Holmes just looked at her. There was nothing to say.

And so began the loops and the stags, and then Johnny Wadd was born. Holmes let his hair grow, started wearing three-piece suits. He and Sharon settled into a strange hybrid of domesticity. She paid for food and household expenses, did his laundry, cooked for him when he was home. Holmes kept his porn money and spent it on himself. By 1973, Holmes and Sharon were sharing the same house, even the same bed, but they were no longer

having sex. Sharon had gone so far as to stop physical relations, but she couldn't bring herself to kick him out. "Let's face it," she says. "I loved the schmuck. I just didn't like what he was doing."

Holmes bought himself an El Camino pickup and a large diamond solitaire that became his trademark in films. Then he designed a massive gold and diamond ring in the shape of a dragonfly. The ring covered his finger from knuckle to knuckle. He wore it on the third finger of his right hand. Whenever he had a few extra thousand bucks, Holmes would add more wings to the dragonfly, more diamonds. Working with his Armenian jeweler, he also designed a gold belt buckle, measuring eight by five inches. The buckle depicted a mother whale swimming in the ocean, her baby nursing beneath. Holmes was into Save the Whales. He wore the buckle when he and Sharon sold bumper stickers door-to-door.

In 1974, Sharon became the resident manager of a ten-unit apartment court in Glendale. It was owned by the pediatrician she worked for; she and Holmes lived rent-free in an adjacent house. Sometimes he worked around the apartments as the handyman and gardener. He also renovated the house, outdoing himself in the master bathroom, recreating a backwoods outhouse, complete with a quarter-moon cutout, a shingled roof over the bathtub and a rough-hewn box around the commode. Bathrooms were a thing with Holmes. "Anything John had to tell you that he knew you wouldn't like he told you in the bathroom, a place where there was a sense of filth and a sense of cleanliness," Sharon says. "You go into the bathroom, do your thing, get rid of the waste, then you clean up, right? This is how he was. He wanted to give you the bad news, then flush it away." Holmes would be in the bathtub many years later when Dawn finally decided to run away. He was also in the bathtub when he told Sharon what he knew about the mass murder that would eventually transpire on Wonderland Avenue.

Holmes was an inveterate collector of junk. He picked wire out of dumpsters and sold the copper. He went to garage sales and bought old furniture. He could repair anything. If a chair was

MARILYN CHAMBERS

is

InSatiable

Also Starring
SERENA · JOHN LESLIE · JESIE ST. JAMES
MIKE RANGER · DAVID MORRIS · RICHARD PACHECO
Featuring
JOHN C. HOLMES

Produced and Directed by
GODFREY DANIELS

Recording sung by
MARILYN CHAMBERS

A MIRACLE FILM Release

Ⓧ NO ONE UNDER 18 ADMITTED

missing one rocker, he could mold a new one. He was a talented artist who sketched and worked in clay. He collected antique pistols, knives, toy soldiers, skulls. He got the heads from taxidermists, then boiled them down himself, in a pot on Sharon's stove. He had a cow, a pig, a coyote, and a bear. Once, according to Sharon, he somehow got UCLA to give him a human head. He boiled it down. They called it Louise. At Christmas, they decorated it with colored lights.

About this time, Sharon says, Holmes also began working as a courier for the Mob. "He'd come home from one of his movie premières, take off his boots, peel down his socks and take out a wad of large bills. He'd say, 'Count this.' We're talking $56,000 in two boots, his Fryes. His famous Fryes. He'd be doing an engagement in Chicago, New Jersey, Miami, New York. It was tied into the film premiers and promos of his films. A lot of the theaters were Mob connected. I'd count the money. He'd take some out for himself, then deliver the rest."

Dawn Schiller arrived in Holmes' life in 1976. She was a teenager, and her parents had just divorced. She'd driven out from Miami with her father and younger sister. Along the way, in Colorado, Mr. Schiller picked up a hitchhiker who was going to Glendale to see his girlfriend. Mr. Schiller had no particular plan; Glendale sounded just fine. By the time they pulled into the apartment complex managed by Sharon Holmes, it had been decided. The Schillers would stay there.

The place had ten free-standing cabana apartments, built around a courtyard. Holmes' half-brother and his wife lived there; this little community was the personal fiefdom of John Holmes. One day, Dawn was visiting a neighbor named Harriett when Holmes came by to deliver a bag of pot. Holmes hung out a while and talked. At one point he asked her how old she was. When told she was fifteen, Holmes looked her up and down appreciatively and said, "Too bad you're so young."

"You know who that was?" Harriet asked Dawn excitedly after Holmes left. She took Dawn over to a closet. Inside was a collection of John Holmes movie posters. Dawn didn't quite understand. She'd never even *heard* of porn. At first she thought Harriet was saying that Holmes was a big Hollywood actor. *What does he mean I'm so young?* she asked herself, a bit indignant, a young girl who was soon to grow up fast.

And so the courtship of Dawn began. Whenever Holmes returned from days or weeks away, he would bring gifts: stuffed animals, roses, a ring. For her sister, Terry, fourteen and over-weight, he brought what they called "Terry food," pounds and pounds of candy. Holmes hired the sisters to do gardening around the complex. When they'd finish work, he'd make them sandwiches. Holmes had a van by then, and soon he began organizing camping trips with Dawn, Terry and Terry's boyfriend, Jose. "I was really charmed," Dawn says. "I was just taken off my feet. He treated me very special." Holmes was thirty-one, sixteen years her senior.

One night Holmes told Dawn to meet him at the van. They went to the beach. "I didn't know what was going to happen, but I knew what might," she says. "We sat on the rocks, the moon was just right. We sat for a long time, and he was very, very quiet. He just stared. I played in the water. When I got out, he said, 'Let's go,' and we drove toward home. And then, just as we got to this intersection, he slammed on the brakes. It was dark, and there wasn't any traffic. He said, 'Would you make love to me?' I literally shook to death. I said yes. I loved him. We did it in the van. After that I was his."

In time, Dawn's father went back to Miami and took Terry with him, and Dawn moved in with Holmes' half-brother and his wife, David and Karen Holmes. Dawn dropped out of Glendale High School. During the day, she worked in a nursing home. At night, she baby-sat for David and Karen.

By 1978, Holmes was freebasing cocaine all the time. He was turned on to the drug on a movie set in Las Vegas and had been smoking ever since. Now he never went anywhere without his brown Samsonite briefcase. Inside were his drugs, his glass pipe, and baking soda and a petri dish for cooking cocaine powder

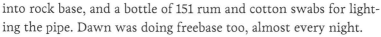

into rock base, and a bottle of 151 rum and cotton swabs for lighting the pipe. Dawn was doing freebase too, almost every night.

"When he did coke," Dawn says, "he'd do it until it was all gone, and then he'd scrape the pipe and smoke all the resin he could find, and then he'd take a bunch of Valium. He'd have me make these peanut-butter chocolate-chip brown-sugar butter cookies. All the sugar helped him come down. He'd have a big glass of milk, and we'd turn on the cartoons, and then he'd go to bed in Sharon's room. I'd usually fall asleep on the couch."

By this time, Sharon had befriended Dawn. "The poor girl was emaciated," Sharon says. Sharon moved Dawn out of Karen and David's and into a garage apartment in the complex. A few months later, Dawn moved into the guest room of the house. "I knew the whole picture," Sharon says. "I knew what was going on with her and John. What he was trying to do was establish the earlier marriage type of relationship where he was my whole life. But I grew up, he did not. So he was trying to remake it with Dawn. He was picking on a kid that didn't know any better. I had to let her know there was another world out there, that John was not God almighty.

"Dawn and I developed a genuine friendship. I showed her by example. I taught her how to cook. Now, of course, John was terrified that I was going to confront her. But I had no reason to confront her. Why? Why would I confront her? He meant nothing to me in that way. He was another human being and that was it, as far as I was concerned. But she was a human being and had equal rights, and I felt she had the right to realize that there was something else going on."

Holmes was gone now more and more, making films in Europe, San Francisco, and Hawaii; doing private tricks; traveling to film openings across the country. At the same time, Holmes was acting as an informant on matters of porn and prostitution for Sergeant Tom Blake, an LA vice detective. He began spilling to Blake in 1973, after he was arrested on a movie set. It is debatable whether Holmes ever told Blake anything he could use.

Also during this period Holmes spent much of his time with his best and only friend, Bill Amerson, in Sherman Oaks. Amerson was an ex-football player, a former stunt man. His specialty was crashing motorcycles. He worked in such movies as *Hell's Angels '69*, and *The Glory Stompers*, with Dennis Hopper. Now Amerson was writing, directing, and producing porn. He and Holmes had met on a shoot in San Francisco in 1970 where Amerson was directing. He had heard Holmes was arrogant, a prima donna. The first thing he said to Holmes, who was playing a hand of poker on the set with some other actors at the time, was this: "If you don't get your ass out of this chair right now, I'm gonna kick the shit out of you in front of all these people."

Amerson went six-four, 250 pounds.

Holmes was holding three queens.

He folded.

"That's how we started," says Amerson. "John was like a little brother to me. He saw the stability. He always wanted to be like me. I'm the only man he ever respected in his life."

Amerson named Holmes the godfather of his children and gave Holmes a key to the hillside tract house and his own room. Holmes and Amerson went hunting, deep-sea fishing, camping in Yosemite. Once, Amerson remembers, Holmes hacked off part of his little finger with a machete while trying to impress some girls with his fire-building skills. Holmes watched LA Kings hockey, and any football; he could sit on the couch through the weekend into Monday night watching college and pro games. He was the world's worst gambler. In Vegas, he'd lose ten or fifteen grand. Then he'd get lucky and win a pot. Then he'd start crowing about his "system" and lose it all again, Amerson says.

Most of Amerson's activities with Holmes excluded women. "John didn't particularly care for women," Amerson says. "At times, I think, he disliked women. He would rather be out in the woods. He was really a simple kid. He liked going to Disneyland, he liked all the rides. A big thing for him, believe it or not, was his bubble pipe. I'd come home and there would be soap bubbles all over his room. I'm probably the only one who ever saw John

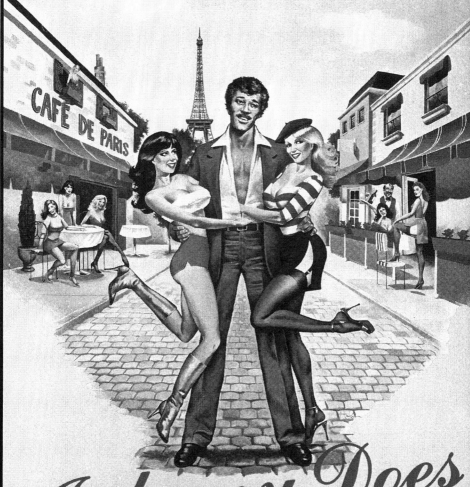

AN AMERICAN STUD IN PARIS
John Holmes Gives Lessons In Love The French Way!!

CAFÉ DE PARIS

Johnny Does Paris

Starring JOHN HOLMES • GLORIA LEONARD
Also Starring DELANIA RAFFINO • JACQUES GATO • BETSY WARD
With FRANCOISE VADIM • JEANNE RAMBAUD • JACQUES MARBEUF
MARGUERITE DARC • BRIDGETT PARC
PLUS A SUPER-LUSTY SUPPPORTING CAST OF FRENCH FOXES!
A VALIANT INTERNATIONAL PICTURE

ADMISSION RESTRICTED

cry. He was really sensitive, but he didn't want anyone to know. A puppy getting hit by a car, a dead bird, strange things made him cry. We spent hours talking about reincarnation, about life, about God—or the lack of God."

Holmes started to become erratic around 1978. On sets, he was harder and harder to deal with. He'd lock himself in bathrooms, in closets. People who worked with him joked that you had to leave a trail of freebase from the bathroom to the bedroom to get Holmes to work. He took so much Valium to level out the jangle of the coke that he'd sometimes fall asleep while an actress was working on his penis. Amerson would get calls from directors. He'd go to the set, usually a rented house in the San Fernando Valley. He'd find Holmes "going through drawers, looking for something to steal. He'd turned into a fucking burglar." One night, while at Amerson's, Holmes suggested burglarizing the house next door. It belonged to an assistant district attorney.

"John got strange," Amerson says. "He'd talk about weird things. He couldn't hold a conversation for very long. He got wild eyed. He didn't make a lot of sense when he talked."

Finally, Holmes had to quit doing films. "When he first started freebasing, as far as the sexual thing goes," Amerson says, "well, cocaine does a funny thing to you. It makes you think you're Superman for the first eight months. And then all of a sudden, you get fucked up one night and you're going to fuck the world, and your dick doesn't talk to you. And you wonder what happened. It's almost like your dick laughs at you. 'Ha! I got you! I ain't working no more.' And that's what happened to John. He kept doing more and more base. He kept getting more and more fucked up, thinking the more he did, maybe that would get it going. After a while, it didn't matter anymore. He was so fucked up it didn't make a difference."

Soon the man who once claimed to be making almost $500,000 a year selling his sexual charms was working as a drug delivery boy for the gang of outlaws and junkies who lived on Wonderland Avenue. He stole luggage, broke into cars, visited old girlfriends and tricks and ripped them off, charged $30,000 worth of appliances to Sharon's credit cards and fenced them for cash. For a while, he and his half-brother David tried to make a go of a combination antique store and locksmith service. Dawn ran the store, which Holmes named the Just Looking Emporium. They decorated the place during all-night coke sessions.

After a few months Holmes began losing interest in the store, as everything else. He'd walk through the door with his briefcase full of paraphernalia and go straight to the bathroom. In those days, a user had to cook his freebase himself—freebase being a purer, unadulterated form of coke that is similar to crack but more potent (crack manufacturers would later use what adulterants called "blow up" to increase the volume of the product). Depending upon the purity of the drugs, when a user cooked a gram of cocaine—a simple process using water, powder cocaine, baking soda, and a source of heat—he got back maybe forty percent, four or five big hits of pure, concentrated, unadulterated coke that would light up the genitals and make the ears ring. Grams at the time went for $100. A decent eightball (3.5 grams) sold for about $150-$200. Holmes was smoking a hit of freebase every ten or fifteen minutes. It was becoming more and more expensive as his tolerance grew. Inventory began to go missing from the shop. Then Holmes was gone for a while. David started bossing Dawn around, accusing her of sleeping with other men.

Holmes finally returned the night the store closed its doors for good. Strung out and paranoid, he reiterated his brother's charges of infidelity. "That was the first night he punched the shit out of me," she says. "He said I was having all these affairs, and I thought, *How blind can you be? I'm living only for you.*

Thereafter, the beatings became regular. "He blackened my eyes, he tried to poke my eyes out, he stabbed me, he threw me on glass, kicked me in the ribs till they were broken. One time he beat me so I'd sleep with these two black guys from his answering service. I think he couldn't pay the bill. Then he beat me 'cause I slept with them. Here was a man who helped little old ladies across the street. *Literally.* We'd come to an intersection, and he'd help this little old lady cross the street. And this is what he was doing to me. He was no longer the man I'd first fallen in love with."

During Christmas of 1979, Holmes' mother, Mary, came to visit. Though Sharon and Holmes and Dawn tried to act like nothing was remiss, Mary caught wind of the drugs and the affair with the underage girl and fled the house, screeching as she left that Dawn was "the devil." Soon after, Holmes and Dawn moved out of the complex for good. They stayed in motels sometimes, but mostly they lived in Sharon's Chevy Malibu, which Holmes had appropriated. Dawn spent even more time in the car. "I was famous for waiting in the car," she says. "We'd drive somewhere to do a drug deal. He'd get out. I'd wait. Sometimes it would be two days. I'd have a six-pack of Pepsi and a coffee can to pee in. And my dog, Thor. He was a little Chihuahua. John and Sharon gave him to me. I was a champion waiter. I know I sat in front of the house on Wonderland Avenue many times, but he never let me go in. I never met anyone until I started doing tricks."

Soon Holmes moved Dawn, now twenty, into an apartment in the Valley with a porn actress and high-priced hooker named Michelle. Other actresses/hookers lived in the complex too. "All these girls were junkies," Dawn says. "They were shooting speed every day. This black girl, Frosty, she was so hardcore. One day she couldn't find a vein and she asked for my help. I was freaking out. Finally, we tied off her tit and found a vein. I remember cleaning her up with a cotton ball."

In the early hours of January 14, 1981, Dawn and Michelle were visiting an apartment in a fancy complex in Marina Del Ray. A regular customer of Michelle's had requested a session with two women; in the trade it was called "doing a double." Holmes acted as the driver. While Holmes was waiting for them in the parking lot, he took the opportunity to break into a van and steal an $8,400 Savin computer typewriter. Thus far, Holmes had been pretty lucky. His connection as an informant to LAPD Administrative vice detective Tom Blake had kept him clear of being busted. But now Holmes was committing larcenies and felonies almost every day.

As luck would have it, the girls returned to the car at about 2:30 a.m., the same time as a police squad car happened to make a somewhat-regular patrol through the parking lot. Noting the suspicious activity—two girls dressed in spangly late-disco era outfits, driven by a scraggly guy in a Malibu strewn with clothes and possessions—police searched the car and found the computer in the trunk.

Holmes told the cops he'd found the expensive computer in a dumpster ten days earlier, while delivering antiques to a client. Michelle told the cops that a friend of hers had given the computer to Holmes that afternoon. Dawn just broke down and cried. All three were taken to jail.

Holmes called Eddie Nash to bail them out.

Back on the street the next day, Dawn told Holmes she didn't want to go back to Michelle's, so Holmes took her to Sharon's house in Glendale. The locks had been changed, but Dawn crawled through the dog door and let Holmes in. They took clothes and canned goods, went back to Michelle's. At the last moment, when Dawn refused to go inside, Holmes punched her in the stomach and dragged her forcibly through the door.

After they'd settled in, Holmes announced that he was going to take a hot bath.

"Get some sleep," he ordered Dawn. "You gotta work tonight."

Sitting in their bedroom in a stupor, exhausted by drugs and prostitution, the general whirlwind of their life, Dawn listened to the water run. Then the spigot squealed, the water turned off. She could hear Holmes entering the water, the small splash, the cleansing *ahhhhh.*

I'm gonna run. She told herself. She'd had enough. *The time is now.*

She was halfway out the door of the small apartment when she heard his voice through the bathroom door: "Honey, get me a cup of coffee, will you?"

She froze, took a step back inside, toward the kitchen.

WHEN JOHNNY WADD SEES A WOMAN HE WANTS, HE TAKES HER!

TELL THEM JOHNNY WADD IS HERE

Starring JOHN C. HOLMES as JOHNNY WADD

Also starring FELECIA SANDA - VERONICA TAYLOR - JOAN DEVLON -
Guest Star ANNETTE HAVEN | Special Guest Appearance by CARLOS TOBALINA |
With PAUL STIFFLERIN - MICHELLE SCHERR - CANDICE CHAMBERS
Screenplay by ROBERT MATHEWS - Executive Producer R. ALDRICH
Produced by DAMON CHRISTIAN - Directed by BOB CHINN

EASTMAN
COLOR

X ADULTS ONL

"Okay, baby," she called down the hall.

Then she took a deep breath and slipped out the door.

Cradling Thor in her arms, Dawn ran to a nearby Denny's restaurant. A little old man lent her a quarter. She called her mother in Oregon, asked for a bus ticket. Mom said okay, but the whole transaction couldn't happen until the next day. Dawn cried. The man bought her a bowl of chili, offered to sneak her into his nursing home. Dawn slept the night on the floor by his bed. Later she would say that he fondled her ass, but that the price was worth it. With that kind of compromise she'd kept herself alive since an early age. At least she was free from Holmes.

Word of the old man's visitor spread through the old folks home. Some of the residents were scandalized. Others were charmed. In the morning, they brought offerings of food from the cafeteria.

When Dawn called the Glendale bus station asking for information, the ticket agent she spoke with was very nice too. In the course of a few minutes she opened up to the stranger, explaining that John Holmes, the porn star, was looking for her and wanted to kill her. The agent drove to Denny's to pick her up. After Dawn's bus left, Holmes showed up as expected at the bus station. The ticket agent played dumb. He told Holmes that a girl meeting that description had gone to San Francisco. Holmes followed the bus the entire way, nearly eight hours' drive.

On the night of June 28, 1981, the Wonderland Gang, in a stolen Ford Grenada with only fumes left in the gas tank, driven by McCourt, drove over the Mulholland Mountains on Laurel Canyon Boulevard and turned right onto Dona Lola Place. They parked in the cul-de-sac in view of the house and cut the engine. They'd just passed Holmes, who'd given them the thumbs up. The sliding door to Eddie Nash's guest bedroom house was still unlocked as planned.

DeVerell, Lind, and Launius pushed aside the chain-linked gate to Nash's driveway, a rather downscale choice of fencing material for the neighborhood, and filed around to the right, behind the house. They went inside, opened the interior door, peered out into the hallway. Lind took the lead with a short-barreled .357 Magnum in one hand, a stolen San Francisco police detective's badge in the other. They found Diles and Nash in the living room. Diles was wearing sweatpants, carrying a breakfast tray. Nash was wearing blue bikini briefs.

"Freeze!" Lind yelled. "You're under arrest! Police officers!"

DeVerell and Launius covered Nash. Lind made his way behind the shirtless, blubbery bodyguard. Lind shifted the badge to his gun hand, his left, then took out the handcuffs with his right. As Lind fumbled with his paraphernalia and Diles' thick wrists, Launius moved closer to help... and tripped, bumping into Lind's arm. The gun discharged. Diles was burned with the muzzle flash. The right side of his back, over the area of his kidney, began to bleed. Nash fell to his knees. He begged to say a prayer for his children.

"Fuck your children!" Launius said. "Take us to the drugs."

While Lind rolled Diles like a walrus onto his stomach, handcuffed him, and threw a Persian rug over his head, the others took Nash to the master bedroom. Everything was exactly where Holmes had said it would be. Lind put his .357 to Nash's head, asked for the combination to the floor safe. Nash refused. Then Launius forced the stainless-steel barrel of his gun into Nash's mouth. The proud Palestinian, known for killing anyone who crossed him, sobbed and relented.

Inside the floor safe were two large Zip-lock bags full of cocaine. In a gray attaché case were cash and jewelry. In a petty-cash box were several thousand Quaaludes and more cocaine. On the dresser was a laboratory vial about three-quarters full of heroin.

"Is that all of it?" Launius asked.

"Yes, yes," Nash said, still on his knees.

"Bullshit. Where's the rest?" Launius pointed the gun at Nash's crotch.

"In the attic. A paper bag. Cash," Nash whimpered.

DeVerell went to the attic. Lind taped Nash's hands behind

his back, put a sheet over his head. He found a Browning 9 milli-meter under Nash's bed, then went to Diles' room, where he found a sawed-off shotgun, two antique rifles, and the two antique pistols Holmes had some weeks earlier given Nash on behalf of the gang as collateral.

On their way out, Launius asked Lind for the hunting knife he always carried on his belt, biker style. He went over to Diles, pulled the four-by-five rug off his head, edged the knife against his neck.

"Where's the rest of the fucking heroin?" he demanded. To a junkie, nothing appealed more than the promise of a huge pile of his drug of choice.

Diles refused to say. Launius pulled the knife slowly across the big man's fleshy neck. Blood flowed.

Outside, McCourt began honking the horn of the getaway car.

"Forget it!" Lind said. "Let's get out of here."

Lind, McCourt, Launius, and DeVerell waltzed through the door of the Wonderland house at about 10 in the morning, laden with booty from the heist. Their spirits were high; they'd just ripped off a major player. Their caper had gone off with nary a hitch. The proceeds included three pistols, the two antique rifles wrapped in a white plastic shower curtain, a gray briefcase, and a metal strong box containing cocaine, Quaaludes, heroin, cash, and jewelry.

Holmes jumped up from the couch. "You did it! Great! That's good!" he enthused.

"No thanks to you, donkey dick," McCourt said. He and Holmes were the two lowest on the pecking order.

Holmes ignored him. "So what happened?" he asked the others. "How did it go down?"

"Don't tell him nothing," Lind snapped. He, Launius, and DeVerell went to Launius' bedroom and shut the door. According to the original plan, these three gang members—the three who'd actually carried out the robbery—were each to receive twenty-five percent of the booty. Holmes and McCourt would go halves on the last quarter. However, the three had decided, before leaving Nash's, that they would short Holmes and McCourt in the division of the loot. Working quickly, Launius removed about $100,000 in cash from the briefcase and hid it in his room.

Meanwhile, Joy Miller and Barbara Richardson, Lind's girlfriend, left the house and drove down the hill to the Laurel Canyon Country Store. Miller was the leaseholder of the three-story stucco house at 8763 Wonderland. She was DeVerell's girlfriend. Richardson was Lind's girlfriend. She'd come down from Sacramento with him a month earlier, was staying with him at the house while he and the others did robberies and drugs. Newly flush with cash, the women bought everyone cartons of cigarettes, then filled the empty gas tank of the getaway car.

When the women returned, the men were at the glass table in the breakfast nook. Everyone was busy. Holmes and Lind were weighing the cocaine. Launius was counting the Quaaludes. DeVerell counted the money. In total, they had eight pounds of cocaine, five thousand Quaaludes, a kilo of high-quality China White heroin and $10,000 in cash. The jewelry would later be fenced for $150,000.

As soon as the weighing was done, Holmes went to the kitchen to cook some cocaine powder into rock. Holmes was a very efficient cook. He used a petri dish instead of a spoon or jar like other folks. Miller and DeVerell called him Betty Crocker. Nobody at Wonderland really liked Holmes. They had no respect for him. When they'd met him two years earlier, he was big man, a porn star. Now he was nothing more than a thief and a drug addict like them, and he wasn't even as good at it as they were. At this point, they were just about done with him.

When Holmes finished cooking, he took his rock and his glass pipe and went, as usual, to the bathroom to smoke. The rest of the Wonderland people took turns injecting heroin and cocaine. After a while, Holmes came out into the living room. Emboldened by the fresh hits, he complained about his share of the money. It was only about three thousand dollars. He knew

DONALD U. CUNARD
Presents

AROUND THE WORLD

X

WITH

JOHN "The Wadd" HOLMES

STARRING

JOHN HOLMES

WRITTEN, PRODUCED & DIRECTED BY

DONALD U. CUNARD

CINEMATOGRAPHY	ASSISTANT DIRECTOR
JORDAN GOODMAN	DAFFODIL CUNARD
LIGHTING	SOUND
ROXANNE, S.P.L.L.	AMERICAN PHONICS, INC.
MUSIC	JEWELRY
LEROY DAVIDSON	CALICO OF BEVERLY HILLS

Location Directors

SAN FRANCISCO	JACK COOPER
LAS VEGAS	VALERIE DAMON
NEW YORK CITY	UPTOWN PROD.
LONDON	SIR DAVID CHATTSWORTH (Thames River Prod.)
PARIS	M. JACQUES PIERRE BOVÉ
ROMA	ANTONIO CONDOTTI

that his friend Eddie Nash had a lot more than ten grand lying around the house.

An argument ensued. Launius punched Holmes in the stomach. Then he hit Holmes with his own Blackthorn walking stick, an expensive affectation he'd lifted from someone and insisted on carrying from time to time.

"Get the fuck out of here!" Launius screamed.

For the first few months while she was in Oregon with her mother, Dawn refused to take Holmes' calls. She got a job at a nursing home and was paying her mom rent, trying to rebuild her life. But Holmes kept calling. He sent flowers, presents, photos of them with the dog, photos of them at Christmas. He wrote long letters begging her to see him one more time. "Just one last look at you," he wrote, cribbing the words from a then-popular song Barbara Streisand had sung to Kris Kristofferson in the popular remake of the movie *A Star Is Born*.

By May, Dawn began to weaken; the pair started talking again on the phone. He told her he was off drugs. He promised never to hit her again. He promised no more prostitution. By June, she was thinking, "Well, I'm not doing anything here. My mom's making me pay rent. It'll be different this time, I'm sure of it."

On June 27, two days before the Wonderland Gang robbed Nash, Dawn flew to Los Angeles to reunite with her first love.

Holmes was carrying two suitcases when he met her.

Oh, shit, she thought, but she didn't say anything. "I didn't want to believe I'd fallen for a line again," Dawn says. "He was sweet. He was great. There wasn't any trouble. We went to a motel, had a nice reunion. No drugs. It was really nice. He was like the old John. Then he left."

On the day of the robbery Holmes still hadn't come back. Management asked Dawn to leave because Holmes hadn't paid for the room.

Dawn had no money. She packed her suitcase, gathered up her Chihuahua. She didn't know what to do. She couldn't call

Sharon. They hadn't spoken in two years. The motel was downtown. She didn't know where, exactly. She walked the streets, tried to think.

A pimp tried to pick her up. Then another. Then she ran into a woman preaching fire and brimstone on a corner. The woman latched onto Dawn; clearly this was a soul in need of salvation. The woman took her to her house, put her to work painting a wall. Meanwhile, Dawn called Holmes' answering service and left the number.

Holmes finally called on the afternoon of the twenty-ninth, after the Wonderland Gang kicked him out. He showed up at the house in the early evening. "He had the biggest pile of coke I'd ever seen in my entire life," Dawn says. "And lots of money. He took over the kitchen. He cooked coke all night long. He even had the holy roller's sister smoking."

In the morning, they went out to get food.

"When we came back, the door was locked," Dawn says. "The holy roller was up in the balcony, waving a Christian flag, praying and hollering, singing 'We Shall Overcome.' John had been using an old tarot card to shovel the coke; she believed it was a sign from the devil. I told her, 'Please, just let me get my clothes and my dog and we'll leave.'"

Gregory DeWitt Diles, six feet four, 300 pounds, barged through the front door of Eddie Nash's house on Dona Lola Place, dragging John Holmes by the scruff of his collar.

As usual there was a party in progress, though things were a little subdued. The Wonderland Gang had stolen almost eight pounds of cocaine. Two customers were waiting. Nash was agitated. They were agitated. In all the time they'd known Eddie Nash, scoring had never been a problem. The supply had always seemed endless.

"What should I do with him, Eddie?" Diles asked.

"In here," Nash said, indicating his bedroom.

Once inside, Nash shut the door.

Diles shoved Holmes to the carpet, prostrate at Nash's feet.

It was Wednesday afternoon, July 1, two days after the robbery. Dawn was tucked into another hotel in the Valley. An hour earlier, in a liquor store, Holmes had run into Diles. As it happened, Diles noticed that Holmes was wearing a ring that had been stolen from the boss... by the Wonderland Gang.

Nash's real name was Adel Gharib Nasrallah. He was a naturalized American, a Christian Palestinian from the West Bank city of Ramallah, who'd come to California by way of Lebanon in 1951. He was fifty-two years old, six feet tall, gray-haired, wiry. His family had owned several hotels before the creation of Israel in 1948. Nash told a friend that he missed the moonlight and the olive trees of his homeland, that he'd spent time in a refugee camp, and that his brother-in-law had been shot by Israeli soldiers.

The youngest son in the family, Nash told people he'd arrived in America with seven dollars in his pocket. He worked for others for a time; he also tried his hand at acting, landing a small part in the television series *The Cisco Kid*. Later he opened Beef's Chuck, a hot-dog stand on Hollywood Boulevard. Nash was on the job day and night, wearing a tall white chef's hat, waiting tables himself.

June M. Schuyler, an elementary-school teacher from Santa Barbara, remembers meeting the "nice-looking, very light-skinned foreign man" at Beef's Chuck. She was living in Hollywood while her autistic son attended the Belle Dubnoff School for Educational Therapy. The school was a block away from Nash's place. She'd often take her son there for lunch.

In a letter to a judge many years later, Schuyler wrote: "Ed Nasrallah began a courtship that was as old-fashioned as they come. For many months he took me out to dinner, introduced me to his mother and other relatives. There never was a sexual relationship between us. I said 'No' and I meant it... Ed told me he had had his fill of loose-moraled women. He wanted a woman he could trust, one he could marry, one who would be the mother of the children he so desperately wanted. He wanted to marry me and he let me know it. (I think he had a small

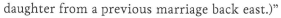

daughter from a previous marriage back east.)"

Over the next year, Nasrallah brought Schuyler gifts of stuffed grape leaves, hummus, and other delicacies. "He had a good sense of humor and we kidded the heck out of each other," Schuyler wrote. When Nash caught tonsillitis from her son, he told her he was going to give her a certificate that said: "The only girl Ed Nasrallah ever went out with in his life and all he got was tonsillitis!" Schuyler said that Nasrallah loved her son exceedingly and that he offered to "fix it up for you to take him to a top brain surgeon. No strings attached."

Nasrallah, she also wrote, was warm, humble, caring. He supported "a whole tribe of family and friends… He spoke of being determined to help other Arabians come over here. Ed Nasrallah came from fine stock, and in 1961 he was basically good."

By the midseventies, Ed Nasrallah had morphed into Eddie Nash and had amassed a fortune. According to court documents, he held thirty-six liquor licenses, owned downtown real estate and other assets worth over $30 million.

Nash was also a drug dealer and a heavy user. His drug of choice was freebase; sometimes he mixed the coke with heroin to cut the edge. According to court documents, Nash was missing part of his sinus cavity, one of his lungs had been removed, and he had a steel plate in his head.

For the last several years, according to court documents, Nash had rarely left his white stone ranch house in Studio City. Just over the hill from Hollywood, Dona Lola Place was nestled into the downward slope of the Santa Monica Mountains, just above the San Fernando Valley. The house was not special from the outside, a typical up-market tract house, but it had all the amenities: three bedrooms, a sunken living room, a bar, a theater-sized TV, plush carpet, mirrors on the walls. Nash was a connoisseur of art; he was well known around the galleries in LA. He had an oil painting by Rembrandt and other valuable pieces. He collected jade, ivory, crystal, silver. Much of his furniture was valuable baroque antique. At home, Nash walked around in a maroon silk robe, or sometimes in bikini briefs, his body covered with a thin sheen of sweat. His voice had a smooth, Arabic lilt. "You want to play baseball?" he'd ask his ever-present guests and customers, lighting his butane torch, offering a hit off his glass pipe.

"The consumption of alcohol and drugs was an ongoing, everyday affair," says an attorney who is a longtime acquaintance of Nash's. "The cast of characters would go from two or three to ten or more. It was amazing, the haphazard way in which people would come and go. You'd walk into the house, there were various girls walking around in various states of undress. Some were quite attractive. Others looked like they'd been sucking on the pipe a little too long.

"When you met with Eddie, you met at his place, on his terms. In those days, I don't think he was functional to drive. He needed to be close to his security. He had to be close to his pipe. I believe that cocaine paranoia created within him the desire to stay within the closed environment that he had control over. If anything, one of the themes in Eddie's life has always been control. He wanted to be in charge. He wanted to be the Arab man in his tent. The master, the giver of hospitality. All his lawyers—I think he had maybe six or seven working on different things—all his managers, employees, customers, everyone, would come to him. He'd have Jimmie, the cook, prepare these elaborate spreads. You could walk up, whisper something in his ear, and he'd make it available. *Whatever.* You just had to ask, and he'd give."

According to court testimony, Nash had a fancy for young girls, whips, and Russian roulette. One woman who had sex with Nash remembers "a lot of temptation. There were piles of cocaine in front of you. Jewelry, wads of money. You'd be left in a room for hours, and then you'd be called in. There were two-way mirrors in the bedroom. In a way Eddie would assess you on what you took or didn't take."

In early 1981, Nash's second wife—the mother of his two sons, aged eight and five—filed for a protection order against

"... An extremely sensuous and obsessively erotic film"
—*Hustler Magazine*

"As beautiful to look at and arousing to remember as any sex film I've seen. I'd gladly lose sleep for Delania Raffino. A luscious film that'll spark your dreams."
MANNY NEUHAUS, *Swank*

"Bring your wife, your lover, your secretary to see "EXTREME CLOSE-UP." Erotic, sensual and as beautiful in the extremes."
Al Goldstein's Magazine

"EXTREME CLOSE·UP"

Ⓧ

High Society's
STARRING
GLORIA LEONARD, JOHN C. HOLMES, DELANIA RAFFINO, JAMIE GILLIS,
PRODUCED BY AARON LINN, DIRECTED BY CHARLES WEBB,
IN EASTMAN COLOR ADULTS ONLY Ⓧ

Nash. When she told Nash she was divorcing him, according to a court affidavit, Nash said, "If you hire an attorney I'll kill you." After she left him, according to a court affidavit, "I took the children to Oklahoma to my aunt and uncle's farm, together with my parents. My husband hired a girl to follow us. She came to the farm to find out if a certain man was with me. After she left, my husband called on the telephone at the farm and said to come home immediately. When I refused, he said, 'Don't come back to California or I will have two men waiting at the airport to kill you, and I will have your parents killed.' He also said that if he wanted to he could have had all of us killed that night."

Nash is said to have had political, police, and crime connections. According to one Los Angeles law enforcement official, "Ed had a lot of contacts. We have to assume at this point that some of those contacts were probably influential people. I'm not saying that these people covered his actions or did anything for him, but Ed Nash was a very well-known figure in the sixties around Hollywood with police, and it was never an antagonistic relationship." Nash's attorney-friend says that Nash "knew and would be seen with people with political influence, with legal influence."

One of Nash's friends and overnight guests was, according to a law enforcement official, an Israeli with a military background, "the so-called reputed godfather of the Israeli Mafia." A report by the California State Department of Justice revealed that the Israeli Mafia was active in California during the late seventies and early eighties and was involved in drugs, arson, extortion, gun-running and a number of murders, including the death and dismemberment of two Israeli nationals at the plush Bonaventure Hotel in downtown LA. The bodies, according to police, were removed from the hotel in a large suitcase and a garment bag purchased at an expensive store in the lobby. Parts of the victims, including the woman's head, were found in four large trash bins in Sherman Oaks. Despite best efforts, police could only locate a single piece of the man.

"Inevitably," said Nash's lawyer friend, "when you're in his kind of business, you're going to deal with patrons, employees, restaurant people. These people are not blue bloods. I think because of Eddie's fast success, people were willing to attribute that to something other than hard work. This business about the Mafia, mob connections, it wasn't necessarily valid, but after a while, things came to have a sort of common acceptance among people. For Eddie, it was a fairly heady experience to have all the success, the wealth. He was a personage. He was important. He was known. In the park he played ball in, he was a star.

"I saw his weakness, his vulnerability, his humanity," said the attorney, who is well connected in Los Angeles politics. "He was giving money to charity, political candidates, just like any other businessman. Most of the time he did it through other people or other names. He was a sucker for a sob story. People would bring someone up to him. You know, this girl is from out of town and she got left by her boyfriend. And I'd see him peel off a couple hundred bucks for her to get a room and get herself together. Eddie was a man's man. He had honor. If he told you he would do something, it would be done. You could rely absolutely on that."

During his six or seven years of heavy drug use, said the attorney friend, "Nash lost over a million a year directly attributable to drugs. I'm not talking about businesses that shut down because he was inattentive, or businesses that were lost because he was whacked out. All that occurred. His business empire totally atrophied as a result of the coke. What really cracks me up is people believed he was a dope dealer. That's bullshit. He was consuming it. At an alarming rate."

On the afternoon of Wednesday, July 1, 1981, Eddie Nash was again consuming drugs at an alarming rate. He'd been ripped off for eight pounds of cocaine, but the Wonderland Gang hadn't found his private stash, and now he was bubbling his glass pipe furiously. He'd sent two of his minions out to score more drugs, but they hadn't yet returned. Two customers waited. They did hits off Eddie's pipe, meanwhile eyeing the door.

One of the customers present in the house was Scott Thorson. At the time, Thorson was the live-in lover of the entertainer Liberace, the rhinestone piano queen of Las Vegas. He was also in Liberace's act. Thorson had been with Liberace since he was a teenager. In the act, Thorson wore jewel bedecked livery. He would chauffeur Liberace onto the stage in a glittering, mini-Rolls Royce, open the door, take his master's fur coat. Then Liberace would make a joke about having the only fur coat in the world that had its own limo. During one special engagement, Thorson danced with the Rockettes. Liberace called him Booper, treated him like a son, a lover, a pet, a progeny.

Thorson had been addicted to cocaine for several years. It began, according to Thorson's autobiography, *Behind the Candelabra*, when Liberace ordered him to have cosmetic surgery. The aging star was concerned about his own fading looks. He decided to preserve his own image on the canvas of Thorson's young face. Before the surgery could proceed, Thorson writes, he had to lose thirty pounds. A doctor of dubious practice prescribed a salad of different drugs to aid the weight loss. Pharmaceutical cocaine was one of the ingredients.

In time, the surgery was completed, and Thorson was made into a young vision of Liberace. But he remained addicted to coke. When Diles barged through the door with Holmes in tow, Thorson was with Eddie in his bedroom, doing hits, waiting to re-up his own personal stash. Nash was very upset. The Wonderland Gang had put him on his knees, made him beg for his life. They'd stuck a gun in his mouth, tied him up, put a sheet over his head. Shot his body guard. Stole jewelry, money, and drugs. Humiliated him in his own home.

"I'll have them on their knees!" Nash ranted to Thorson. "I'll teach them a lesson! They'll never steal from anyone again!"

Thorson was excused. Nash closed the door. Diles smacked Holmes, threw him across the room, shoved him against a wall, and then down to the carpet at Nash's feet.

"How could you do this thing!" Eddie Nash screamed. Diles

kicked Holmes in the gut. "I trusted you! I gave you everything!"

Nash and Holmes had met three years earlier at the Seven Seas, another of Nash's clubs. Holmes was on his way to San Francisco to shoot a film, and his regular connection, a member of the Lavender Hill Mob, LA's gay mafia, was unavailable. Nash was glad to help; he was a huge fan of porn. He'd even invested in several movies, leased office space to a number of porn-related operations. Holmes was one of the greats in the business. Nash liked having him around. Nash introduced him proudly to all his guests: "I'd like you to meet Mr. John Holmes," he'd say. In terms of connections, they'd been together a long time.

For his part, Holmes did anything he could for Nash. Holmes thought Nash was the most evil man he'd ever met, but he couldn't quite figure him out, so he respected him. He also respected his drug supply. Frequently Holmes brought women to Nash, porn stars and innocents, too. On Christmas Day 1980, he'd even presented him with his precious Dawn. Nash reciprocated with a quarter ounce of coke.

Now, however, things weren't so chummy. Holmes was crumpled on the floor. Diles had pulled out a gun; he held it to Holmes' head. Nash leafed through a little black address book that Diles had taken from Holmes' pocket.

"Who's this in Ohio?" Nash screamed. "Who's Mary? Your *mother*? Who's this in Montana? Is this your *brother*? I will kill your whole family! All of them!

"Go back to that house!" Nash ordered Holmes. "Get my property! Bring me their eyeballs! Bring me their eyeballs in a bag, and I will forget what you have done to me! Go!"

Thursday, July 2, 3:30 a.m. Sharon Holmes switched on the porch light, spied through the peephole.

Christ, she thought, *It's John!*

She hadn't seen her husband in three months. His clothes were ripped, he was bloody from head to toe. He stared straight ahead, unblinking. She opened the door.

John didn't say anything.

Sharon folded her arms across her chest. "Well? What do you want?"

"Accident… car… um…" he stammered. "Can I… come in?"

They went to the bathroom. Many years before, when he'd renovated the house, John had outdone himself on the bathroom, creating a kind of indoor outhouse. Everything was still perfectly in place, down to the half-moon cut-out in the door.

Sharon, a registered nurse, rummaged through a well-stocked medicine cabinet, brought out iodine and cotton swabs. She reached up and took Holmes' chin in her hand, turned his head side to side. *Funny*, she thought, *No cuts, no abrasions. Just blood.* "You had an accident in the Malibu?" she asked him. It was, after all, still *her* car.

Holmes looked at Sharon. His eyes blinked rapidly. They'd been married sixteen years. Sharon always knew when he was lying. That's probably why he always came back. "Run me a bath, will you, please?"

Holmes eased into the tub. Sharon sat on the wood-covered commode. *What now?* she thought. He dunked his head, put a steaming washcloth over his face. Then he sat up. "The murders," he said. "I was there."

"What do you mean, you 'were there'?"

"It was my fault," Holmes said. His eyes welled. "I stood there and watched them kill those people."

"What are you talking about?"

"I was involved in a robbery," Holmes began, and he told the story. The setup, the robbery. Nash's threat to kill his whole family, Sharon included. "So I told him *everything*," Holmes said. "I told where the robbers lived and how to get there. I had to take them there."

"Who?"

"Three men and myself."

"Okay, you took them there."

"I took them there. There was a security system at the

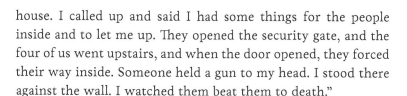

house. I called up and said I had some things for the people inside and to let me up. They opened the security gate, and the four of us went upstairs, and when the door opened, they forced their way inside. Someone held a gun to my head. I stood there against the wall. I watched them beat them to death."

"You stood there?"

"There was nothing I could do."

"John, how could you?"

"It was them or me. They were stupid. They were dirt."

"What do you mean? They were people who trusted you."

"The guy they robbed, he was a big guy. He was evil. The most evil man I've ever known. And they robbed him and slapped him around and made him beg for his life. They deserved what they got."

"Blood! Blood! So much blood!"

Holmes was having a nightmare. Tossing and moaning, punching and kicking. "So much blood!" he groaned over and over. "Oh God, so much blood!"

In bed with him in their motel room, Dawn was scared to death. She didn't know what to do. Wake him? Let him scream?

It was Thursday, July 2, 1981. After bathing at Sharon's, Holmes had come here, to this motel in the Valley. He walked through the door, flopped on the bed, passed out.

Dawn sat very still, watching a TV mounted on the wall. After a while, the evening news came on. The top story was something about a mass murder. The cops were calling it the "Four on the Floor Murders." Dead were Joy Miller, Billy DeVerell, Ron Launius, and Barbara Richardson. Four from the Wonderland Gang. Dawn stood up, moved closer to the tube. *That house looks familar*, she thought. And then things started to click. *Waitaminute! I've been there! Isn't that where John gets his drugs?*

Hours passed; John woke. Dawn said nothing; they went and got McDonalds, came back and watched some more TV. Then came the late news. The murder weapon, it was reported, had been a steel pipe with threading at the ends. There were

All Men Between the Ages of 18·75

I WANT YOU!
TO ENLIST IN THE ARMY OF LOVE
AN EXCEPTIONAL FILM FOR ADULTS ONLY
STARRING JOHN (JOHNNY WADD) HOLMES AND USHI

IN VIVID COLOR   RATED XXX

thread marks on the walls, on the victims' skin and bones. The house was tossed by assailants who seemed to be searching for something. Blood and brains were splattered everywhere, even on the ceilings.

The bodies were discovered by workmen employed next door after hearing faint cries from the back of the house—"Help me. Help me." A fifth victim was carried out alive. Her name was Susan Launius. She was twenty-five, Ron Launius' wife. She hadn't seen him in months. He'd called after the robbery and told her to come by. Things were going to be better, he promised. Now she was in intensive care with a severed finger and brain damage. Police were comparing the case to the Sharon Tate murders by the Manson Family.

Holmes and Dawn watched from the bed. Dawn was afraid to look at Holmes. She cut her eyes slowly, caught his profile. He was frozen, the color drained from his face.

Then the weather report came on. Dawn cleared her throat. "John?"

"What?"

"You had this dream. You know, when you were sleeping? You said something about blood."

Holmes' eyes bulged. He looked very scared. She'd never seen him look scared before.

"Yeah, well, uh," he said. He smiled his smarmy fake smile, which was meant to be reassuring but was not. "It's nothing. I hit myself yesterday when I lifted the trunk of the car. I gave myself a nosebleed, wasn't that stupid. It's nothing, don't worry."

On July 10, police knocked down the door of their motel room and arrested Dawn and Holmes. For the next three days, Holmes, Dawn, and Sharon were held in protective custody in a luxury hotel in downtown Los Angeles. There were armed guards in the lobby and in the hallway outside the door. Holmes and his party were allowed all the room service they wanted while Holmes maneuvered to make a deal with the cops. He wanted witness protection, a new name, money, a house. He wanted new names for Sharon and Dawn. He offered to tell the police secrets only he knew: He'd name names of mobsters, drug dealers, prostitutes, and pimps, he promised them.

But all the police wanted to know was who killed the Wonderland Gang.

Holmes wouldn't tell.

"The whole time he was in custody, it was like Holmes was on center stage and the lights and the camera were on," says a detective who was present. "It was like he was doing a movie. Here he is, he has two women with him. All three of them are sleeping in the same bed. He stoked us, jacked us around. He told us certain things. That we were on the right track, that this is indeed what had happened, that this was the motivation, that this was how it came down. He played it for all it was worth, then he said he wouldn't testify. We had no choice to cut him loose."

The three went back to Sharon's house. Sharon cooked dinner. Holmes picked up Sharon's two dogs and Thor from the kennel. Later, the women dyed Holmes' hair black. Using cans of spray paint, Holmes and Dawn painted the Malibu gray with a red top. The finish was drippy and streaked.

At midnight they were ready to go. Having bought provisions for the drive, the Malibu was parked in the parking lot outside the Safeway in Glendale, near Sharon's complex. The engine was idling. Dawn sat in the front seat with Thor in her arms. Holmes leaned up against the back bumper, smoking a cigarette. Sharon stood just beyond arms' reach, hugging herself protectively, as people do.

"Change your mind, Sharon. Come with us."

"No way, John."

"It can be the three of us, Sharon, like old times."

"You've got to be joking."

"You can't do this to me," he said.

"Why? Why can't I?"

"Because I love you."

Sharon stared up at him. On their first date, he'd brought a bottle of Mateus and a handful of flowers. Sharon had watched through her window as he picked them from the neighbor's front yard. Now she shook her head, no. *What a wasted life*, she thought. She walked around the car to the passenger side. Dawn leaned out the window and they hugged. Over the years, as odd as it may seem, they'd become close, like mother and daughter.

"Take care of him," Sharon said.

After leaving California, Dawn and Holmes went to Vegas, where they gambled at the roulette tables at the Aladdin. Next they visited John's sister in Montana, where the couple hunted, fished, and took long walks in the woods. During this whole time, there were no drugs. It felt to Dawn like she had the old John back. Then one day his mother called from Ohio. The FBI had been there looking for him. The couple took off on the lam again, heading south. They visited the Grand Canyon, drove through the Painted Desert. To finance the trip, Holmes broke into cars along the way. In Oklahoma, they were stopped by a cop for speeding, but he let them go.

The couple ended up in Miami, at a small run-down hotel on Collins Avenue called the Fountainhead. Everyone there was on some kind of slide. Big Rosie, the manager, let Dawn work the switchboard and clean rooms in exchange for rent. Holmes went to work for a construction company, painting a hotel down the strip.

For extra money, Dawn solicited tricks on the beach. "He told me how to do it," she says. "It was amazing. He said, 'Just wear your shorts and your bathing suit top and walk on the beach.' And I'll be damned if I didn't get propositioned. I still don't know how. To me, of course you're wearing a bathing suit on the beach. I didn't even know we were in that area. He had a smell for it or something, a sense. It was his life. He recognized it.

"Everybody at the hotel got to know us," Dawn says. "We were real friendly. John was doing a lot of drawing. Drawings of the dog, of me. We'd have dinner with other people at the hotel, go to movies. We were like a normal couple. After a while, I said

I didn't want to go out on the beach anymore. He'd *promised* when I came back that I wouldn't have to. So we had a big fight and I ran out of the room, down to the pool, and he ran after me, the fool. He caught up to me in front of the snack bar. Everybody was down there, everybody we knew. He grabbed me by the hair, got me on the ground. And he just beat the shit out of me. Then he just sort of dusted himself off and walked back up to the room. Everybody was just shocked. They didn't know that side of him. That wasn't the John they knew. He was the real kind guy. He'd do anything for you. He had a heart of gold. Right."

The next day, while Holmes was at work, a delegation of residents came to see Dawn. A mother and daughter offered to help. The daughter had a kid and a job. She was moving to a house. Would Dawn want to be the live-in baby sitter? Dawn packed her bag, gathered up Thor, put Holmes' gun in her pocketbook.

Two weeks passed. She neither saw nor heard anything from Holmes. Then, on the morning of December 4, the phone rang. She picked it up.

"Hello, Dawn."

It was her brother Chris. He was sixteen and lived in Oregon with her mom. She hadn't heard from him in, what, six months? Not since she was home, at least.

"How are you, Sis?"

"Fine. Where are you calling from? You sound close."

"I'm here."

"In Miami?"

"Yeah."

"What are you doing *here?*"

"Well, I, I, ah, came... with a friend. Listen. Tell me where you are. I'll come pick you up."

Dawn hung up the phone. Immediately she knew something weird was going on. Chris didn't have a driver's license. How could he rent a car and come pick her up?

Chris showed up on foot. They bought a six-pack at a convenience store and went to a nearby park, sat by a pond. For a while they chit chatted and caught up.

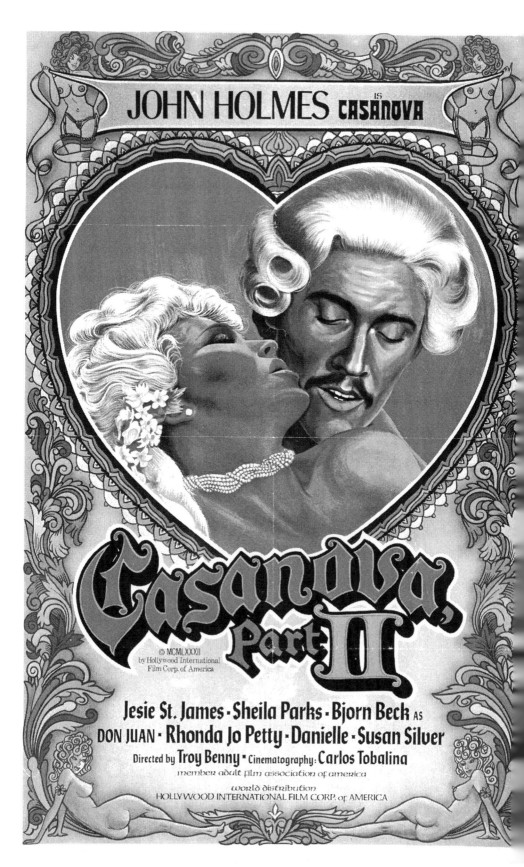

Then Chris got quiet. "See that car over there?" He pointed toward the parking lot. "It's the cops."

Angered by another betrayal, blindsided again, Dawn stood and began walking away.

Chris caught up and grabbed her elbow. "Listen," he said, "people are after John, and they think you're with him. You're going to get hurt. Tell the cops what they want to know, 'cause otherwise John's going to be dead in a few days. There's no way around it. You're probably going to be saving him."

Brother and sister walked over to the cops. The detectives convinced her it was in her best interest to give up Holmes' location. Searching her big purse for the address of the Fountainhead, she became overwhelmed and began to cry. As if in slow motion, she sat down in place on the asphalt.

Sobbing, she continued to rummage through her purse for the address. She took out some makeup, put it on the ground next to her. She took out a pack of gum, some rolling papers, a compact... a gun.

All three cops drew their weapons. Dawn looked up distractedly, like, *huh?*

Then she realized. She'd been carrying it around for so long that it just felt like normal life.

She smiled weakly, picked up the pistol and handed it over.

When the cops got to his hotel, Holmes was there. "I've been expecting you," he said dramatically, as if speaking a line from one of his old Wadd films. Ever the cool cat, he invited them in for coffee.

"How you doing, John?" said the man in the gray suit, leaning over the safety rail of the bed. "John? Do you remember me?"

It was February 1988, seven years after the murders, a sunny room in the Veterans Administration Hospital in Sepulveda, California. The man in the suit was LAPD detective Tom Lange. In later years his face would become well known as one of the team of investigators assigned to the O. J. Simpson/Nichole Brown Simpson murder investigation. Behind him was his partner, Mac McClain. The case of the Wonderland murders was still open. They had a few questions for John Holmes.

"We want to talk to you about Eddie Nash," said McClain. "John? Do you remember Eddie? John? Are you awake?"

Holmes' eyelids fluttered. He weighed ninety pounds. His fingernails were two inches long. He was dying.

Following his arrest in Miami, Holmes was tried for the murder of the Wonderland Gang. His lawyer's defense was simple: John Holmes was the "sixth victim" of the Wonderland murders, and Eddie Nash was "evil incarnate."

"Ladies and gentlemen," his lawyer told the jury at the outset, "unlike some mysteries, this is not going to be a question of 'Who done it?' This is going to be a question of 'Why aren't the perpetrators here?'"

In the end, the most damaging evidence the prosecution could produce was a palm print on a headboard above one of the victims. Holmes did not testify. The jury found him innocent.

Holmes remained in jail, however, on his outstanding burglary case. While awaiting that trial, he was ordered by a judge to tell the grand jury what he knew about the Wonderland murders. Because he'd already been tried for those murders and could not be tried again, according to the U.S. constitution, Holmes would not be able to invoke the Fifth Amendment. By law, he had to talk. But Holmes refused. He'd underestimated Nash once; he'd never do it again. Nash would kill him and his family if he talked, he was certain of it.

Holmes was held in the county jail for contempt. His lawyers, meanwhile, battled in the courts over constitutional semantics. Holmes was being confined for not talking, and he'd said he never would. The question was this: at what point did confinement cease to be legal punishment and begin to be illegal coercion?

While incarcerated, Holmes went on a hunger strike. Two weeks later, it was reported that he'd lost only seven pounds and that jailers said other inmates were sneaking him candy bars. Later it was reported that on several occasions Holmes had

interrupted his fast, eaten a meal, and then resumed his fast.

Finally, on the afternoon of November 22, 1982, Holmes relented and testified. He'd been in jail eleven months in all, 110 days on the contempt charge. His attorney told reporters that he'd changed his mind because of "certain arrangements" that had been made and "certain circumstances" that had arisen. What he may have been referring to was the imprisonment, that very same morning, of Eddie Nash, on charges of dealing drugs.

After the Wonderland murders, Nash and Diles were put under intense scrutiny. Nash's house was raided three times. The busts were carried out by the combined forces of a SWAT team, homicide and narcotics detectives, and federal agents from the Drug Enforcement Agency and the Bureau of Alcohol, Tobacco and Firearms. Each time, drugs, money and weapons were seized. Each time, Nash made bail. Then Nash was arrested with three others on federal charges of racketeering, arson and mail fraud, an insurance scam. Nash's three coconspirators were found guilty. Nash was acquitted.

In the end, both Diles and Nash went to jail. Diles got seven years on charges stemming from the drug raids. Nash was found guilty of possessing two pounds of cocaine for sale. At trial, his lawyer argued that the $1 million worth of coke was not for dealing, that it was strictly for personal use. A psychologist from UCLA testified that Nash had been freebasing two to three ounces of cocaine every day for the last five years. During recesses in the trial, Nash would go out to his car and smoke freebase. Then he'd swallow a few Quaaludes and return. His lawyer hired a young associate to sit at the defense table next to Nash. He was instructed to stick Nash with a pin whenever he nodded off.

The judge in the case was Everett E. Ricks Jr. It was obvious from his comments that Ricks, a hard-liner, considered Eddie Nash a plague. Ricks even came in to work from his sickbed especially to sentence Nash. Coughing into the microphone, Ricks called Nash "a danger to the public" and maxed him out. He was given eight years in prison and a $120,350 fine.

EXHAUSTED

JOHN C. HOLMES

THE
REAL
STORY

STARRING **JOHN C. HOLMES**   RATED X

WITH THE BIGGEST GALAXY OF STARS EVER ASSEMBLED IN ONE FILM

ALSO STARRING	SEKA	ANNETTE HAVEN	JESSE ST. JAMES	GEORGINA SPELVIN	LINDA WONG
	LAURIEN DOMINIQUE	EILEEN WELLS	CHRIS CASSIDY	FELICIA SANDA	KITTY SHANE
	BONNIE HOLIDAY	CHRISTIN SARVER	FATIMA HAMMOUD	MELBA BRUCE	CANDICE CHAMBERS
	JESSICA TEMPLE-SMITH	FAY BURD	PHARDRE KYOTO	JENNIFER RICHARDS	MONIQUE STARR

and introducing **LAURIE SMITH** and **LAURA TOLEDO**

PRODUCED AND DIRECTED BY
JULIA ST. VINCENT

INCLUDING WORKS FROM DIRECTOR
BOB CHINN

ASSOCIATE PRODUCER
LEE KASPER

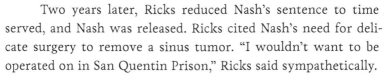

Two years later, Ricks reduced Nash's sentence to time served, and Nash was released. Ricks cited Nash's need for delicate surgery to remove a sinus tumor. "I wouldn't want to be operated on in San Quentin Prison," Ricks said sympathetically.

And two years after that, Ricks was held against his will for psychiatric observation. The fifty-two-year-old, now retired, had been arrested after he allegedly punched his eighty-two-year-old mother and threatened to kill someone if she didn't give him keys to a car.

After his release, Nash moved to a modest townhouse condo in Tarzana, just north of the Hollywood Freeway, and began taking college business courses at night. Nash told a friend that jail had saved his life. He set about rebuilding. Drugs, inattention, back taxes, and lawyers' fees had depleted his fortune considerably, as had the legal battles with his daughter.

According to court records, Debra Marie Nasrallah Amidich, also known as Debbie Nash, was Nash's daughter by his first marriage. She was twenty-seven and unemployed when Nash went to jail in 1982. Debbie, who hadn't seen her father in twenty years, flew out from Wisconsin to visit. She told him she had read about his drug trial in the paper, but "didn't care what they said about him." She wanted to be his daughter, use his name, stand by him in any way she could. A few weeks later, Debbie had Nash sign an irrevocable power of attorney. It gave her absolute control of everything he owned.

In time, Debbie stopped her weekly visits to Nash. She wouldn't take his collect calls, stopped paying the bills. An inspection of the Seven Seas turned up mold, maggots, flooding, and drug paraphernalia, and soon the building went into foreclosure. The parents of Debbie's boyfriend attempted to purchase it. Finally, Nash's brother Schel Nasrallah, also known as Sam Nash, filed in court to take control from Debbie. Affidavits say Debbie threatened to kill her uncle and his family, and that Sam ousted Debbie from the Seven Seas at gunpoint. When Nash was released, the suit was dropped. The matter was settled out of court. Debbie's two-year tenure, according to an attorney, cost

Nash more than $2 million in cash, gold, diamonds, jade, liquor, fine art, and other negotiable assets.

Holmes, meanwhile, had gone back to making films.

When he finally got out of jail, Holmes was jubilant. He greeted reporters, had dinner with his lawyer, then called Sharon. She told him to "get the fuck out of my life." He couldn't call Dawn. She was nowhere to be found. Later it would turn out that she was traveling outside the country with her father, with whom she had reunited.

Holmes had nothing to do and nowhere to go. His lawyer lent him a Volkswagen Beetle and $100, and Holmes showed up at the Sherman Oaks home of his old friend Amerson. While Holmes was in jail, Amerson had started a company called John Holmes Productions. He was marketing Holmes' old films on video. Like all porn actors, Holmes had been paid per day and had signed away the rights to his own films. His old friend was happy to pick them up. "Let's face it," Amerson says, "films are a product. John was a product. I marketed him. Every company utilized John and the films he made to line their own pockets. That's what it's all about. It's business." Amerson gave him his own room in his house.

With all the publicity from the murders, John Holmes had achieved almost mainstream celebrity. The video boom was just beginning, and Holmes became a kind of Marlon Brando of porn. No longer the leading man, he was the featured oddity. In *California Valley Girls*, for example, he had one scene. He enters a living room, sits on the couch. A girl enters stage right and goes to work. Then another girl. Another. By the end, there are six of them at once, working on separate areas of his celebrated member.

Early in 1983, Holmes was shooting the film *Fleshpond* at a studio in San Francisco. One of the actresses in the cast was Laurie Rose. Laurie was nineteen; she came from a small town outside Vegas. In the business she was billed as Misty Dawn; she was known around the business as the anal queen of porn. It was only natural that she was excited to be on the same set as the man they called the King.

"That first time, we didn't get to work together," Laurie says, "but we were attracted. It sounds silly, but you know how you can meet someone for the first time and it's like you know them already? That's how it was. He was charming, very charming, and charismatic. I was having some problems on the set with some girls. They were from New York. They were very rough. They didn't like me too much. They were doing drugs and trying to accuse me of ripping things off from the locker room. They wanted to cut me up. John came up and told them, 'You're not going to touch her.'"

After the film, the gallant Holmes asked Laurie to come home with him to Amerson's. Holmes old friend couldn't help but notice this new girl's resemblance to Dawn; others would later take notice as well. For their first two "dates," Holmes and Laurie smoked freebase and had sex. Then, Laurie says, "the third time I went up there, he came up to me with the mirror and said, 'You want a hit?' and I turned to him and said no. He looked shocked. He said, 'Why not?' and I said, 'Because it makes me feel funny and I can't talk.' So he went in the bathroom, and locked himself in. He stayed in there like three hours, and I'm just sitting there, you know, twiddling my thumbs. Finally he came out and said, 'You know what? This stuff makes me feel funny too. I'm going to quit.'"

In time, Holmes and Laurie moved in together at Amerson's. When Amerson raised the rent to $400, they got their own place in Encino. Holmes continued to make films, but he made Laurie stop. "He thought one porn person in the family was enough. Plus he made more money at it than I did, and didn't like me working. He was jealous but he wouldn't admit it," she says. "And the AIDS thing was just starting to come out. Nobody had gotten it yet, but it was still in the back of our minds. He thought, 'Well, if I'm going to take a chance, that's enough. I don't want you taking a chance, too.'"

Apparently, Holmes had made good on his promise and stopped doing drugs. Holmes and Laurie settled into domestic routine. They cooked dinners, stayed home a lot, watched videos. Holmes liked movies like *Alien* and *The Return of Bruce Lee*. "He was really into fine acting," says Laurie. "If it was a B-rated movie, he would turn it off in an instant." On weekends they went to swap meets and yard sales.

"He was a homebody. Nobody ever came over," Laurie says. "Nobody knew where we lived. His words to me were 'Friends can get you killed.' We were very careful. He was worried about Eddie. He didn't like to carry a gun around with him, but he always had some sort of knife. He carried it in his boot. When Eddie Nash got out of jail, John was very, very worried. We went on twenty-four-hour watch. For like three weeks, one of us had to be awake at all times. It was like being in a movie or something. Kind of dramatic. We had guns. We would have watches. I wasn't working at the time, and he was, so I basically had the night watch."

By late 1984, Holmes was working as an executive at Amerson's VCX films. He was supposed to be doing sales and preproduction, writing and editing, in addition to acting. Amerson says Holmes spent most of his time playing cards and shooting darts. When VCX cut off Holmes' salary, Amerson put up money to start Penguin Productions. Holmes was to run it. Laurie worked as a secretary. "John was tired of the whole industry," she says. "He wanted to make a million dollars so we could just leave and be done with it. John had a spot picked out where we could go. He wouldn't tell me where. I know that it wasn't in this country. He wanted to get as far away as he could."

Then, in the summer of 1985, Holmes tested positive for HIV.

"He went fucking crazy," Amerson says. "He was panicking. He said, 'I'm gonna die!' and drove off. We didn't know where he was going. Maybe he was going to kill himself."

"Maybe he was going to look for drugs?" Laurie says. "We didn't know. I was so scared."

Holmes returned to the office a few hours later, his attitude somehow readjusted. "He was laughing about it," Laurie says. "We closed up the office and went to the beach. We played Neil Diamond, Fleetwood Mac, our favorite songs, you know, like "Stairway to Heaven." We walked and walked and talked and talked. John was philosophical. He said he felt like he was chosen to get AIDS because of who he was, how he lived. He felt like he was an example. It's almost like, he always wanted to make his mark on the world, and now he was going to. And even though this wasn't exactly what he had in mind, you know, the world moves in mysterious ways."

Holmes continued to make films, including *The Private Life of John C. Holmes*. The iconic cast included Ginger Lynn, one of the top women of eighties porn; Tracy Lords, who would eventually cross over to minor stardom in legitimate films (and who, it would be revealed, had started her career in porn while still underage); and gay porn star Joey Yale. Yale has since died of AIDS.

Holmes' last movie was *The Rise and Fall of the Roman Empress*, starring Ilona "Ciccolina" Staller, a member of the Italian Parliament. By the time it was released, in 1987, Holmes' health had already begun to slide. The word in the industry was that he had colon cancer. Holmes was telling people that doctors had removed sixteen feet of his large intestine. In truth, Holmes was operated on for hemorrhoids. Around that time, he also began developing complications related to AIDS. Amerson, meanwhile, accused his friend of embezzling $200,000 from the company. He cut Holmes off and canceled his insurance.

"John was really sick by this point," Laurie says. "We moved around a lot because the rent kept going up. I was working as a computer programmer. John would just stay home. He was in so much pain, you couldn't touch him. He couldn't walk. His legs and feet would swell up, his ears would bleed, he had infections in his lungs. His surgery wouldn't heal up, either. He was very upset about the business. He'd made all these people millions and millions of dollars. We were really broke. He called some people, and they said, 'We'll help you out.' But we'd never get the money they promised."

Wadd

THE LIFE & TIMES OF
JOHN C. HOLMES

THE SAGER GROUP PRESENTS
a CASSEL PRODUCTION a FILM BY CASS PALEY
"WADD: THE LIFE & TIMES OF JOHN C. HOLMES"
JOHN C. HOLMES · MISTY DAWN · BOB CHINN · KITTEN NATIVIDAD · MIKE SAGER · RON JEREMY · LARRY FLYNT · P.T. ANDERSON
DIRECTOR OF PHOTOGRAPHY WILLIE BOUDEVIN SOUND JOHN REESE ORIGINAL MUSIC BRAD RAYLIUS DANIEL & TAD DERY
EXECUTIVE PRODUCER RUSS HAMPSHIRE CO-PRODUCED & EDITED BY CHRISTOPHER ROWLAND
PRODUCED & DIRECTED BY CASS PALEY

On January 24, 1988, Holmes and Laurie were married in the Little Chapel of the Flowers in Las Vegas. It was a simple ceremony. The bride wore white. "It was a big ordeal for him," Laurie says. "He knew he was dying. He knew we wouldn't have a life together."

In February, Holmes was admitted to the VA hospital in Sepulveda. Soon after, detectives Lange and McCain called the hospital. They wanted to see Holmes. After seven years, the district attorney was reopening the Wonderland case, based, in part, on testimony from Scott Thorson, Liberace's ex-lover. Thorson, who was waiting to be sentenced on a drug-related armed robbery, had sought a deal with police. He was prepared to testify that Eddie Nash had sent Holmes and Diles to Wonderland Avenue and that Nash felt responsible for the "bloody mess" that resulted. Now the police wanted Holmes' testimony to corroborate.

Laurie was standing at the door to Holmes' hospital room, taking a breather, when she spotted Lange and McClain coming in lockstep down the corridor.

She turned and stage-whispered into the room: "John, they're coming."

Holmes put out his cigarette and closed his eyes.

"He was close to death. Basically incoherent," Lange says.

John Holmes died about a month later, on March 13, 1988.

"It was very peaceful. His eyes were open," Laurie says. "When I walked in the room, it looked like John had sort of looked up to Death and said, 'Here I am.' His face looked peaceful. It was the most peaceful look I ever saw on him in my life. I tried to shut his eyes but they wouldn't stay shut. It was weird because, you know, I was trying to play this role here, like in the movies, when somebody dies with their eyes open. But it didn't work like that. I'm thinking: *Hey, why won't they shut?*"

Holmes didn't want a funeral, but he did have a last wish. "He wanted me to view his body and make sure that all the parts were there," Laurie says. "He didn't want part of him ending up in a jar somewhere. I viewed his body *nekked*, you know, and then I watched them put the lid on the box and put it in the oven. We scattered his ashes over the ocean."

Six months later, on September 8, 1988, Diles and Nash were charged with the murders on Wonderland Avenue. After a preliminary hearing in January 1989, at which Thorson, among others, testified, Nash and Diles were bound over for trial, held without bail in the Los Angeles County Jail. Nash's and Diles' attorneys maintained their clients' innocence and question the credibility of witnesses for the prosecution.

In 1990, Nash was tried in state court for having planned the Wonderland murders; the trial resulted in an 11-1 hung jury. It would later be alleged, in federal racketeering charges brought ten years later against Nash, that he had bribed the lone holdout, a young woman, with $50,000. The retrial of that case ended in an acquittal as well.

The Wonderland investigation eventually ran for ten years and included three trials—but never one conviction. Nash is still alive and living in the Los Angeles area. Diles died in 1995 from liver failure. Susan Launius, the fifth victim, survived the attack and continued with her life. David Lind died of a heroin overdose in 1995. Tracy McCourt died of unspecified causes in 2006. Sharon Holmes died of complications due to Alzheimer's disease in 2012; at her bedside was Dawn Schiller, who has written a memoir, *The Road Through Wonderland: Surviving John Holmes*.

"You know," says Detective Lange, "there's no mystery here. Every time you read something, they say it's a big mystery. Or the local TV says it's a big mystery. Or that show out of New York, you know, *A Current Affair*. Big mystery. Like aliens or something. But there's no mystery. John Holmes didn't go to his grave with anything but a very bad case of AIDS. He told us everything initially, right after it happened.

"But it's one thing to tell someone something," Lange says. "It's another thing to testify to it in court."

Wadd

THE LIFE & TIMES OF
JOHN C. HOLMES

THE SAGER GROUP PRESENTS
A CASSEL PRODUCTION A FILM BY CASS PALEY
"WADD: THE LIFE & TIMES OF JOHN C. HOLMES"
JOHN C. HOLMES · MISTY DAWN · BOB CHINN · KITTEN NATIVIDAD · MIKE SAGER · RON JEREMY · LARRY FLYNT · P.T. ANDERSON
DIRECTOR OF PHOTOGRAPHY WILLIE BOUDEVIN SOUND JOHN REESE ORIGINAL MUSIC BRAD RAYLIUS DANIEL & TAD DERY
EXECUTIVE PRODUCER RUSS HAMPSHIRE CO-PRODUCED & EDITED BY CHRISTOPHER ROWLAND
PRODUCED & DIRECTED BY CASS PALEY

LITTLE GIRL LOST

Savannah was a gorgeous porn starlet, among the first of the luminescent Vivid Girls, with a taste for handsome rock stars, fast cars, expensive designer gowns . . . and copious amounts of drugs to quiet her demons. When things fell apart, she could see only one way out.

J ason slammed the door shut, slumped back against it. His soft brown eyes were saucered with panic; his lightly muscled chest was pumping air. "She did not just do that," he groaned.

He smoothed his fingers down one of his fashionably-trimmed sideburns, absently measuring its length against the bottom of his earlobe, wondering what to do next. He glanced around her closet: Bob Mackie gowns, Anne Klein suits, Chanel shoes, ripped Levi's on individual hangers, hatboxes, dozens of them. "Dude, this isn't happening."

He pushed himself off the door, began pacing the long walk-through closet—five steps forward, turn, five steps back— rerunning the scene in his mind. His knee hurt. What was she thinking? Driving the Corvette like a maniac, squealing around curves, him screaming in the passenger seat - *Slow down! Slow down!*—and the next thing you know, around this one corner, it was so weird, kinda slow motion, he's seeing this fence two inches from his window, this whitewashed fence with big, heavy boards, and she's just plowing it down, splintering board after board after board, the white fiberglass nose of her car crumpling, the awful shattering noise, and then *boom!* she hits the tree.

It was now about 2:30 A.M., July 11, 1994, an hour or so after the accident. Jason Swing paced the closet, forward and back, and then on one trip he continued all the way to the opposite door, the master bathroom. He went in.

The Jacuzzi was swirling, and the candles were lit, dozens of candles, reflected in a three-way makeup mirror. He walked around idly, picking up a false eyelash, a ceramic cat, a bottle of white Zinfandel. He took a swig. Shit! he thought. He coulda been boning by now. His eyes fell upon the view from the sliding-glass doors that made up the north wall of the room, down the slope toward the river of lights on the Hollywood Freeway, and in the distance, up on the hill, the amber glow of Universal City.

Jason took a deep breath, walked back through the closet. He stopped at the door he'd slammed. On the other side was the garage. He called out in a tentative voice: "Shannon? Savannah? Can you hear me?"

He pressed his ear to the door, listened.

Breathing. It sounded like she had asthma or a bad cold.

He opened the door slowly.

Back in time, four years ago, Shannon sitting on a black leather sofa. She's a platinum-blonde, pale as porcelain, arms hugging her knees to her chest, two-inch lacquered nails, her big blue eyes bloodshot and glassy, tears running down her smooth chipmunk cheeks, past her overdrawn red lips... drip, drip, drip, into the deep V neck of her sweater, her new breasts, the work of a Beverly Hills plastic surgeon, 435 cc of saline solution in a silicone pouch on each side, catching and heaving in silent anguish.

She'd been found out, and she knew it, but she didn't know what to do next, so she was doing the usual: nothing. She was a young woman who lived in the moment; there was nowhere else for her to go. When things got bad, this was her reaction: curling into a ball, letting the events flood, waiting to see where she washed up.

Billy sat at her feet, yoga-style on the shag carpet, his palms pressed together as if in prayer: "Come on, Shannon, tell me, babe," he pleaded. "It's okay, sweetie. Let it out."

Billy never knew what to expect. Or maybe he did. She could be so childish and endearing and happy one moment, squeaking and giggling with joy, tilting her head to one side and winking a Maybellined eye, playing with Willie, the kitten—their son, she joked—and then suddenly, the dark curtain would descend, the tears, the silence, the pain. Sometimes, making love, Billy would raise his head and look at her face, so pretty, except for her eyes, glazed and staring like a doll's. Where she had gone he could only imagine.

They had met at the Ventura Theatre eighteen months earlier, the night after Halloween, 1989. Shannon Wilsey was 19, lived with her dad in Ventura, an hour northwest of Hollywood. Shannon worked in a boutique on Main Street, went to the beach every day, studied for her GED. She had posters of rock stars on her walls, a subscription to Guitar Player, liked to dress the family dog in party clothes with her 6-year-old half sister. Five-foot-four, 105 pounds, pert breasts, killer little ass, 34-24-34, Shannon was the kind of girl the Beach Boys had had in mind, the archetype of the California girl, updated with a tiny thong bikini. She had a dozen of them, all the same: the top, two little triangles, with strings around the neck and back; the bottom, a snake of spandex peeking out from the smooth crease of her butt, slithering high over her hips, diving small and tight in front. Just before she met Billy, she'd entered her first bikini contest at the local Holiday Inn. She took third. She blamed her breasts. Her Tater Tots, she called them, giggling, then growing teary. That was before the surgery. Sometimes you can fix what you think is wrong with you. Sometimes not.

Anyway, Billy Sheehan was onstage at the Ventura Theatre playing with his band, Mr. Big, when he spotted her. He was the leader, a garage-product from Buffalo who'd gotten his break playing bass in David Lee Roth's post-Van Halen group. Now Mr. Big was about to tour with Rush; a gold album and a hit video were in Billy's future. Shannon had come especially to see him. "My favorite thing in my little life is rock and roll," Shannon would say in her squeaky-cute, syrup-sweet voice, Marilyn Monroe meets Betty Boop. Her ambition, she told her dad, was to marry a rock star. The notion that someone loved by millions would love only her: Ultimate attention, that was her ideal.

She was in the front row when Billy spotted her, this real, live, perfect Varga doll, right down to the neatly trimmed bangs veiling her forehead. The spotlights sought her out in the shadows like rays from heaven, and she glimmered and shone, an angel dwelling on the outskirts of the mosh pit.

When he awoke the next morning, she was sleeping there beside him, so sweet and so beautiful—the skin, the ass, the tattoo on her ankle, "GREGG." Man, I could spend the rest of my life with this, he thought.

Two months later, at the end of his tour, he called. She sounded surprised.

They reunited at a Denny's on Sunset Boulevard. Shannon waiting at the counter with her bag. For the next few weeks, they played house at Billy's, just having the greatest time. Shannon never talked about her past, never talked about much of anything. What was on TV, who was in concert, what she was doing this moment—that was her world. She seemed simple; she wasn't really. She was just too closed off to let you in. You could tell she was hiding something. You didn't want to know.

In time, Shannon got a little apartment she called the Hellhole, with a roommate but no furniture. Shannon and Billy came and went, he for tours, she for, well, he wasn't quite sure what. She'd just disappear for a few days, a week, then show up again. Maybe if she hadn't been so beautiful, he would have asked. Beauty does that: shuts you up, makes you cling, blinds you to things.

Like countless pretty, young hopefuls before her, Shannon began her Hollywood sojourn with a B movie, *The Invisible Maniac*. She took Billy to the premiere at the Ritz Theater, in August 1990. Billy thought Shannon looked great twelve feet high on the screen. At one point, she had this really cute dumb line, and the whole place roared. Billy thought she was wonderful. "Babe, you are a fucking star," he said. Shannon said nothing. She thought they were laughing at her.

Said the Los Angeles Times: "The youthful actresses bare

their bosoms about every five minutes… The morbid, puritan-
ical effect, axiomatic in schlock exploitation fare, is that sex,
represented by all that bared flesh, just has to trigger a wretched
excess of violence."

Shannon disappeared.

A month later, she showed up at Billy's in hysterics. She told
him this story about how she'd once been involved with rocker
Gregg Allman. He wanted her to make a movie. She had signed a
contract and taken the money, but now she didn't want to do it.

Billy said he'd talk to his lawyers. Shannon grew fright-
ened. "No, no, that's okay," she said. "I just wanted to see what
you thought."

Then she had the breast surgery, and Billy wondered where
the money had come from, but this was, after all, Hollywood. It
wasn't until she pulled up in a brand-new Mustang convertible
that he started asking questions.

"Did you get the money from Gregg Allman?"

"Yeah, and I have money left over." She giggled, so proud.
"You should see my new apartment!"

Soon after, Billy was browsing a newsstand when something called *Squeeze* magazine caught his eye. It cost $16. There
on the cover was Shannon, his baby, wearing the little black
dress he'd bought her. She had a guy's prick in her mouth.

Billy called his partner at Metal Blade Records, who called
his wife, who worked at Flynt Publishing, the home of Hustler.
She asked around.

Shannon had signed a movie deal with Video Exclusives,
a low-end, triple-X distributor. The deal specified twenty-five
pictures, $250 per scene, plus an additional $250 each time she
appeared on a box cover.

Billy called Shannon, sat her down on his leather sofa,
took a place at her feet. "Babe," he said, "I know where you got
that car, the apartment. I know the whole thing…"

"What?" said Shannon.

"Babe," he said, "I know all about the contract."

Deny. Deny. Deny.

"What's going on with you?" he asked. "If you want to do a love scene and show your body, that's okay. But to do a porn movie, babe-this is gonna affect your whole life. Don't do it. Please!"

Shannon went silent, and then the tears began to flow. Billy pleaded with her to talk. "Please, babe. Tell me."

Finally, exasperated, Billy decided to try a little game. He'd been to shrinks. He knew when someone needed one.

"Shannon," he said. "I'm gonna say something, and I want you to answer with the first thing that comes to your mind."

She cut her eyes toward him.

"Why can't you talk, Shannon?" he asked, his voice soothing and professional. "Who's holding you down?"

Shannon's eyes went wide. She blinked. She seemed to go into a trance. It was as if something deep inside had suddenly been unveiled, a dark memory that had eluded her. It was an amazing, sudden transformation. Billy didn't know if she was acting or if it was real. It was like she'd been hypnotized.

"My mom," she said, a soft monotone.

"What's she doing?"

"She's holding me down on the front seat. She doesn't want me. She wishes I wasn't born."

"Where are you driving?"

"To the hospital."

"Why, Shannon? Please, tell me…"

Shannon's mom and dad met in Mission Viejo, California, in the middle of June 1969. Mike Wilsey, 17, was the son of a mailman. He was cruising with a friend in his souped-up VW Bug. Pam Winnett, 16, was the daughter of a nurse and a hippie painter. She was living with her maternal grandparents, hanging out with some girlfriends.

In the late Sixties, Mission Viejo was the frontier of Orange County. The high school had no sports teams, there was no movie theater. It was safe and clean and boring. Shannon Michelle Wilsey was born on October 9, 1970. Mike suspected that the baby was not his, but he and Pam got an apartment anyway, tried to make a go of it.

In Mike's version of the story, he came in time to love Pam, but she was very unstable, very unfaithful. Finally, he couldn't take it any longer. He dropped Pam and the baby at her father's house and said good-bye. Shannon was 3.

Shannon's early memories were disturbing. At the core was the story she told Billy, later others. She was sitting on a beanbag chair in an apartment, she recalled. There was a man dressed in women's clothes. What came next ended with her mom screaming, cursing Shannon's existence, holding her down on the front seat of the car, speeding to the hospital.

After a time, Pam married and moved to Texas. Mike was hurt and angry. "I had been with Shannon long enough to fall in love with her, no matter whose kid she was." But at the same time he was relieved. "I just thought, farewell and good riddance."

Mike's next contact with Shannon was ten years later, when she came to live with him and his wife. The couple were Christians. He worked as a Roto-Rooter man; they lived with their two kids in Oxnard, California. When Shannon showed up, Mike was transfixed. The resemblance was unmistakable. All these years he'd been so sure she wasn't his. His guilt was overwhelming. He prayed.

Shannon was well-behaved at first, but then she started breaking curfew. Mike warned her and warned her. Finally, he turned his 13-year-old daughter over his knee and spanked her.

Shannon went straight back to her mom in Texas. Then she was caught sitting on her stepfather's lap. She was shipped off to her great-grandparents, in Mission Viejo.

So it went, back and forth. One night, in a restaurant in Texas, her mom noticed Gregg Allman a few tables away. "He's staring at you, Shannon. Go talk to him."

Mike's next contact with his daughter was a phone call. "I'm on the road with Gregg Allman," she said. She was 17.

Attorneys for Allman have requested that *GQ* not use his name in connection with Shannon's, but Shannon mentioned it frequently, had it needled into her ankle in blue ink. The details she told of this period were sketchy. Partly because she never told anyone much of anything, partly because it was a haze. She had discovered heroin. She called its effect "the warm fuzzies." Heroin made her feel numb and dreamy, luxurious, safe, timeless. It made her troubles go away.

She traveled around the country when the band was on the road, stayed other times in a high-rise apartment with a private elevator. Gregg came and went. Then there was a big scene with his wife. Shannon called her dad. "I want to come live with you guys."

For the first three months, Shannon adjusted well to family life. She found the job at the boutique, went to night school, kicked back at home.

Soon she became restless. She began going to the Ventura Theater, staying out to all hours. She entered her first bikini contest at the Ventura Holiday Inn.

She finished third that fall night in 1989, and the shoulder she cried on was that of another contestant, Racquel Darrian. Racquel was with her boyfriend and a young photographer named Micky Ray. All three had just started in porn. Micky told Shannon that she was beautiful and that she should be a model. He would do her portfolio, he said, get her a shot with a legitimate agent.

Mike Wilsey suspected the offer, told his daughter she didn't have the background to be an actress or a model. "There's no such thing as 'instant.'" he said. Shannon called Micky. Her dad carried her bags to the curb.

At Micky's, Shannon lay on the couch for days, watching TV, blissed out on some Percodan she'd found in the medicine chest. She kept Micky running out for food, bourbon and cigarettes. They had sex, but she wasn't into it.

Then her dad relayed a message. Billy Sheehan had called.

Shannon got off the couch, asked Micky to drive her to the Denny's on Sunset. She was going to become a star.

A black-tie banquet in a Las Vegas hotel, the 1992 Adult Video News Awards, the Oscars of porn. Light splinters off a mirrored globe on the ceiling, showers the throng below: stars, industry types, pop-eyed fans from across the country, seated at tables of ten, chicken or fish.

Halfway into the program, Chi Chi LaRue has just concluded the entertainment. The six-foot, 300-pound transvestite, real name Larry, is known as the Divine of the industry—a director, gossip columnist, gadfly and chanteuse. Tonight she chose an auburn wig and leather pants with the cheeks cut out. She sang "Spank Me," accompanied by a cavalcade of female stars, a fractured take on a production number: Miss America goes triple-X.

They danced out of the audience, up to the stage, a conga line of porno queens, each one larger than life: bustier, naughtier, with higher heels and deeper necklines, the filmic embodiment of male fantasy and lust. Robin Byrd and Amber Lynn, Christy Canyon, Racquel Darrian, Jeanna Fine, Tori Welles-maybe thirty of them. They spanked Chi Chi's fat pink butt, then turned on one another, swatting and goosing, giggling and mugging and hugging.

And right there, center left, was Shannon Wilsey.

"Where's the bitch Savannah?" called Chi Chi. "She needs a spanking!"

The crowd roared and Savannah stepped forward in her $8,000 Bob Mackie creation, a skintight, low-backed, sequined halter unitard, in rainbow colors with accompanying aquamarine gloves. She could afford the outfit. Savannah was making close to $200,000 a year having sex on film. She sidestepped Chi Chi's swipe, swatted him one.

Now the girls were seated. It was time for more awards. The presenters were two veteran actresses, Shanna and Sharon. The category: best new starlet.

"And the winner is…" they said in festive tandem, opening the envelope. Their faces fell. They emitted a brief, spontaneous moan. "Savannah," they announced.

Accepting her winged golden trophy, Savannah stepped to
the microphone and smiled—a huge, dazzling smile, framed by
red lips. Her eyes were closed; her lids fluttered. Perhaps it was
a shy reaction to all the acclaim or the weight of the two pairs of
false lashes she always wore. Or perhaps it was the Jack Daniel's,
heroin and coke she'd done, her usual cocktail.

"Heeeloo-ooo," she trilled to the crowd in her ditzy way,
her eyelids working open. "Aren't you happy for me?"

She let out a little snort, and then a giggle, and then a long,
whiny laugh, a kid thumbing her nose, tee-hee-hee.

The role for which she'd won was that of Scarlet in *On Trial*,
a film inspired by obscenity prosecutions over the past few years
in small municipalities across the nation. It had been nominated
for eleven awards, including best girl-girl scene, by Savannah
and Jeanna Fine. The film won seven, including best picture.

Up at the podium, Savannah basked in her moment. People
often said she needed a roomful of adulation. Here it was at last.
She lingered at the microphone. "Thank you again," she said
finally. "I love you all."

She blew a kiss, took a step to leave. Then she stopped,
returned to the microphone.

"And if you don't love me, I'm sorry..."

After her first photo shoot with Micky, Shannon tried nudes.
She liked posing, and she liked the money. Soon, she decided to
try films. Her first scene was a girl-girl in *Racquel's Addiction*, with
Racquel Darrian from the bikini contest. Shannon billed herself
as Silver Kane, an allusion to a syringe.

Shannon was two hours late to the set, but when the foot-
age came in, the director was ecstatic. Shannon was the real
thing in a field crowded with almost, not-quite beauties. As to
her performance, well, the camera loved her, and she loved the
camera back, had the self-absorbed exhibitionism of a high-fash-
ioned model. Watching her was like seeing a girl in a jeans
commercial take off her clothes and start having sex.

Only the sex with Shannon wasn't very exciting. Once

that part started, she seemed to excuse herself from her body. If actors sometimes admit to "phoning in" a performance, it would have to be said that Shannon substituted a cardboard cutout of herself. Editors dubbed in the moans and groans.

No matter. They sell fantasy in porn, and Shannon was the ultimate sweet little girl in the parlor, the girl you were hopelessly infatuated with, the girl you could never get. That she didn't act like a whore in the bedroom seemed to fit. It was almost what men expected, a kind of living doll to which you did things.

After two films, Shannon landed the contract with Video Exclusives. The company gave her the new breasts, the apartment on Laurel Canyon and the Mustang. She took the name Savannah from her favorite movie, *Savannah Smiles*, a children's story about a rich little girl who runs away from home and reforms criminals.

The company shot twenty-five scenes but released only ten. Since the advent of the VCR, the porn industry had changed and boomed. No longer relegated to seedy theaters and peep shows, porn films could now be watched in the privacy of people's own homes. By 1993, sales and rentals were at $1.6 billion. At the low end of the market were companies such as Video Exclusives. They pumped out title after title, sex scenes with no plot, something for everyone: black men with white women, women who squirt when they come, shaved pussies, huge breasts, obese people, chicks with dicks.

When her one-year contract was completed, in the fall of 1991, Savannah was sent by Video Exclusives to Vivid Video. Vivid was decidedly upscale, a combination of a modern marketing agency and an old-time Hollywood studio. It signed six very pretty girls a year, made about eight movies with each one, advertised like crazy. Owner Steve Hirsch hired mainstream art directors and fashion photographers for the box covers, spent more than $100,000 a film, allowed six days to shoot a script. Vivid didn't just sell movies. It created porno supermodels, the Cindys and Christys and Kates of triple-X.

Six months into her contract with Vivid, Savannah had done about five films, and Video Exclusives had capitalized, flooding the market with its back catalogue. Savannah was ubiquitous: best new starlet in the industry.

Unfortunately, everyone hated her. They called her "ice queen," "cold bitch," "evil cunt."

They had reasons.

Savannah was by now a $200-a-day junkie. She carried her works in a cloth makeup bag, inside her leather backpack: black-market ten-packs of B-D .29-gauge, ultrafine insulin syringes; the leg from a pair of white tights to tie off her arm; a lacquer-handled tablespoon from Pier 1, charred on the bottom from cooking her brown Mexican tar into a solution.

Savannah had trouble showing up for work. When she did, she was late. Depending on when she'd had her last fix, she was either very animated or very detached. When she began dancing in upscale strip joints across the country, a big moneymaker for porn stars, she never brought along enough drugs. Club owners would find her jonesing on the floor of her dressing room. They'd have to send out a lackey to score for her.

On the set, she was known to be "difficult": "If that goddamn P.A. doesn't get me my coffee in two minutes, I want him fired!"; "I don't want ugly bitches like this in a scene with me!" She demanded script approval, casting approval, her own makeup man. And where was the goddamn ashtray?

They ran and got her an ashtray. The fact was this: Savannah's films outsold all the others' five or six times over—up to 20,000 units each. Whatever Savannah asked for, she got. She responded by demanding more. They responded by hating her more. It was the circle that defined her life.

Savannah liked the acting. She learned her lines, even suggested nuances: "Do you think I should, like, make my voice catch right as I'm saying this?" Her favorite role was the lead in *Sinderella*. On the last day of shooting, the prince didn't show. "It figures," she told the director.

Her sexual performance continued to be mediocre. Most women in the industry say they enjoy the sex, some more so, some less. But they agree that you have to like it a little or you'll lose your mind. You show up for work, and you just let yourself get carried away; you fall in love with your scene partner for as long as it takes to get the film shot. Then you go back home. It's like getting paid for a one-day affair.

Savannah didn't even try to get into the sex. One story had her on all fours on a bed, taking it from behind. Out of the frame, she was absently fingering the leaves of a potted plant on the night table.

"Come on, Savannah," said the director, Paul Thomas. "Say, 'Fuck me' or something."

Savannah looked over her shoulder at the actor inside her. "Fuck me or something," she said, then went back to playing with the plant.

Thomas is Vivid's chief director. He worked with Savannah as much as anybody in the industry did. He echoes the general sentiment: "She was a real bitch. A selfish, selfish bitch. She reveled in putting people down. She didn't like giving of herself in any way, shape or form. She was irresponsible and flaky and selfish and stupid."

In a world of fragile egos and damaged psyches, Savannah made little effort. She rarely socialized with anyone in the industry, though she did often fuck the boss. She was considered the classic ice queen—haughty, distant, unapproachable.

Probably the biggest slight to people in the industry was her mainstream status, the by-product of her penchant for rock stars. Over time, she would be linked with Billy Idol; Vince Neil of Mötley Crüe; David Lee Roth; Danny Boy, leader of the rap group House of Pain; and Axl Rose and Slash, both of Guns N' Roses.

The Star reported Savannah's engagement to Slash: "…and she's flashing a three-carat ring to prove it." People had Savannah and Slash "engaged in full hit whoopee" in a crowded New York club called the Scrap Bar. She was on national television with Marky Mark at the Grammys. And then there was her longest, most publicized affair, with Pauly Shore. He took her to the MTV Video Music Awards, to the opening of the movie *Point Break*, on vacation in Hawaii.

Savannah clipped and saved every article, blacking out any mention of her real name, Shannon Wilsey, with a thick Magic Marker.

Now, at the Adult Video News Awards, Savannah left the stage, made her way through the crowd. She was sitting tonight with her girlfriend Jeanna Fine. They were lovers, fellow junkies. Jeanna was a few years older, a sort of journey woman in the industry who'd worked herself up to become a feature performer.

Jeanna knew Savannah was demanding. Sometimes, when Savannah started her shit—"Hon-eyyy, I'm getting piss-yyy!"— Jeanna would look at her and laugh. " 'Feed me, do me, buy me,'" she'd chant, "the Savannah national anthem." Jeanna had dark hair and dark eyes. Her film persona tended toward dominatrix; at one time she'd done private outcall as such, commanding $1,000 an hour. She could handle Savannah's bullshit, did it well enough to inspire the kind of puppy-dog loyalty of which Savannah was capable when she could muster some trust.

Jeanna said she was "totally, completely, in love with her." She went slowly, got to know Savannah as few did. Jeanna knew how fragile Savannah was, that her bitch thing was really a protective force field, that she was so insecure and needy that her relations with the world were skewed. Jeanna knew about Savannah's passion for fuzzy slippers and macaroni and cheese, and for pink things and flowered sheets and lace. Jeanna knew the way Savannah rubbed her tits all over after she shot up; the way to touch her, to talk to her, to make her moan. Savannah needed constant care. She was dead inside, very lonely. Jeanna pampered her, sometimes ordered her around. Jeanna knew that a woman's clit was really between her eyes.

Now, her moment in the spotlight just passed, Savannah returned to her table to find Jeanna in animated conversation with Amber Lynn. Amber had done three very good years of films, then quit and got into dancing, 800 numbers and products. She was a big name in the business, very well respected among the girls.

Savannah broke into the conversation, turned her back on Amber. "I don't want to hang out with Amber," she whined. "This is my night."

Amber was nonplussed. So this is Savannah, she thought, this surly little kid wearing her mommy's false eyelashes. She's got a few things to learn.

"What's your name?" Amber interrupted. "Shannon? Savannah? Come over here, sit down. Let me talk to you a minute."

Savannah looked Amber up and down, turned on her heel. "Good night, Jeanna," she said.

Up in her room, Savannah sat on the king-sized bed in her spangly outfit. She swigged a bottle of whiskey, snorted a couple lines, set about reading some fan mail.

It was routine stuff—requests for photos and dinner dates, words of longing, poems of lust and admiration, a big thank-you from a wife who said that Savannah's videos had rekindled her sex life. Another envelope:

"Savannah, your terrible. Please retire. Stix R."

She ripped out a sheet of paper, answered in her round, careful schoolgirl print:

Stix,
You don't know me and you never will, all you know is what you see on my movies, which you have obviously taken the time to see in your pathetic "terrible" life. You know you could never be with someone like me. I am the BEST/CLASSIEST woman to ever be in this business. You should feel lucky just to have seen me fuck on film. Get a fucking life, asshole!!! Save your hand for jerking off-not writing stupid letters, you worthless piece of shit.
                                                    Savannah

"Yo," said Jason Swing, answering the black cordless phone, plug-ging the opposite ear with a finger. It was 10 P.M., July 9, 1994. Jason was the personal assistant of Danny Boy. He was house-sit-ting while the white rappers were on tour, livin' large at the star's crib with some buds on a Saturday night.

"Heeeloo-ooo, it's mee-eee!" trilled the voice on the other end of the line.

Jason searched his memory bank. "Me who?"

"Oh. Oh, yeah," said Jason. "Whazz-up?"

Danny Boy was Savannah's latest crush. She'd been in the "Jump Around" video. She was pretty stuck on him. He was noncommittal. It was the pattern.

Ever since Billy Sheehan, Savannah had had a hard time with relationships. Not long after the scene in Billy's living room, Savannah had gone out and fucked Billy Idol. She'd confessed; he'd forgiven. Then she'd started up with a member of Ratt. She'd lied about going to a party Ratt was throwing, forgetting that Mr. Big was on the same label. Billy had stood five feet from Savannah, drinking a beer. She'd pretended he wasn't there.

Savannah wouldn't give her father her phone number; he'd written long letters, in printing similar to hers: "Please don't think I don't care. I do very much. I hope you can talk to me more. I'd like to have your phone number..." Her dad prayed, thought about hiring a private detective. Her mom continued to be indifferent, though Savannah showered her with presents and money. When Savannah had gone home to Justin, Texas, and confessed her heroin addiction, her mom dismissed it as a phase.

Savannah and Jeanna had parted ways after a big scene in Palm Springs. They'd gone there with a sugar daddy. Savannah had been holding the stash of heroin, thirty bags. The girls had had a little spat. Savannah wouldn't give Jeanna her fix; Jeanna refused to beg. While Jeanna was waiting in the hotel lobby for a car to the airport, dope-sick, wishing she were dead, Savannah strutted past in a thong bikini, another girl on her arm.

For a while, there had been Shawn. He was stolen by Savannah's best friend, Julie Smith. The couple had moved into a house that Julie had rented and furnished with a $2,000 loan from Savannah. Then there'd been the married strip-club owner. The last night of a weeklong stint at his club, the two had dinner. He complained about his wife the whole time. When Savannah asked why he'd married such a bitch, he stomped off. He left her with the check, and refused to pay for her week's dancing.

Slash had disavowed their relationship and the "engagement ring." The ring, platinum with three rows of diamond baguettes, was actually from a businessman, during the days when they used to shut his office door for meetings. When she asked that the door remain open, her relations with that company began to sour.

And Pauly Shore? They'd dated for exactly eleven months. Pauly talked about marrying her, the whole sweet nug-and-picket-fence giggage. He also made videos of them having sex. "It just gets to a point where they either move in or you break up," Pauly later said. "I didn't want to get deeper into quicksand."

Now there was Danny Boy, kind of. Jason was the guy who took his messages. Savannah had met Jason a couple of times at Hell's Gate, a club Danny Boy owned with Mickey Rourke and some others.

Jason didn't know Savannah was someone. To him, she was just another blonde party girl with a one-name name and fake tits. Vivid dismissed her in the fall of '92, eight months after she'd won best new starlet. She had her breasts done again, this time with 600 cc of saline in each side, 34DD. She wasn't happy with the work. They wrinkled funny at the cleavage when she leaned over, rippled when she would lie on her back. The scar tissue around the areolae, where the implants had been inserted, was pronounced.

"Is Danny there?" asked Savannah.

"He's on tour in Europe."

"He's gone already?"

"Yeah, he left, like, a week ago."

"Oh," said Savannah, totally deadpan. She was silent a few moments. Then: "What are you doing tonight?"

Jason's father was an interior decorator who'd done Spielberg's house, among others. His mother was an artists' agent. Jason had been a yell-leader in high school in Encino. More recently, he'd gone to cooking school, done club promotions.

Six feet tall, Jason was 22, had soft brown eyes, a matinee idol's dimpled chin, carefully curated sideburns, a black Volkswagen Corrado. He had this clean-cut, Beverly Hills hip-hop white-boy thing going—big pants, sparse goatee, moussed hair with carefree stands, backward baseball cap.

Jason was what they call a Face Boy, a handsome man-child of few words, the male equivalent of the beautiful blonde. He went to all the clubs, knew lots of first names: Arnold, Michael, Mickey, Tori, Pauly and Juliette, on and on. Tonight he was going to a birthday party for—what was his name? One of the two fat guys in the movie *Amongst Friends*, you know, the sidekick guys? One of them.

"A parrr-tyyy?" trilled Savannah, brightening. Already tonight she'd called four people. All of them said they were busy. Last night she'd ended up mudwrestling at the Tropicana for $900. "A party. Realllly?"

She arrived with her Rottweiler, Daisy Mae, in her white Corvette, which had replaced the Mustang. She'd gotten the dog because of a prowler. At first, she'd found flowers trampled around the windows and sliding-glass doors of her house. Then, little things—a watch, a hairbrush—began disappearing. Then she came home one night and all the lights were on and the stereo and TV were blaring: They'd been off when she left. The next day, she went out and bought Daisy. A friend gave her a blue steel .40-caliber semiautomatic Beretta. She kept it by her bed.

Savannah was wearing bib overalls and tennis shoes. She carried a package for Jason: four of her videos, several signed T-shirts, a calendar.

"What are these? asked Jason.

"A little present," said Savannah. "It's me!"

Over the past few weeks, Savannah had been spending quite a lot of time on "me." She'd organized her scrapbook, watched and catalogued and shelved the seventy-four films she'd done, redoubled her efforts to read her fan mail. She set about framing every picture of herself she could find.

After parting with Vivid, Savannah had gone back to Video Exclusives, signed to do twenty-one sex scenes at $4,000 per. By now, the only person in the industry who would or could work with her was Nancy Pera, a.k.a. Nancy Nemo. The birdlike, talkative, fiftyish porn director was a nurturing sort, an old-school Italian mother who'd never had kids of her own.

Nancy called her Savvy—Slash's nickname for her. Whenever Savannah said she needed money, Nancy would organize the scenes, book the sets and choose one of the five men Savvy was willing to work with. Then she'd call Savannah, call her six more times, roust her up, direct and edit the film. Whatever Savannah wanted, Savannah got. Drugs, food, a place on Nancy's couch beneath the knitted comforter when she was too depressed to move. Though some might have seen Nancy as an enabler, she was really more of a hairpin; she held the troubled girl together.

In the summer of 1993, after a boyfriend told Savannah that the needle tracks on her hands and arms were ugly, she decided to kick. She called all over the Valley, collected downers from friends—Valium, Xanax, Seconal, Vicodin—anything to put her out, to wash down with whiskey. One night, she ate so many pills that she passed out on the living-room floor. There were a bunch of people over. They sat around her prostrate body, talking, having cocktails. Savannah would convulse periodically, and then every once in a while she'd sit up, start crying, curse at everybody. Then she'd pass out again.

On the morning of the eighth day, Savannah woke up, took a shower, put on makeup, even her eyelashes. When Nancy came over, Savannah was beaming. "I did it," she said, so proudly.

"Did I really do it? I did, didn't I? I did!"

For the next sixty days, she didn't drink or do drugs. Then she went on the road, dancing. She had vowed to stay off H, but she was scared; she needed something. She told Nancy she had to be fucked up to be slutty, and slutty was her whole routine. Never much of a dancer, she strutted the stage to songs like "Big Balls" and "Bad to the Bone," did the requisite floor work. She drank heavily, took Valium, added a few lines of coke. "Dancing medicine," she called it.

By the late summer of 1993, Savannah had stopped doing movies, but then she got an offer she couldn't refuse. For $9,000, she agreed to appear in *Starbangers 1*, the first in a popular series.

For the first time in her career, Savannah was a consummate professional on the set. Everyone in the industry was talking: Savannah the ice queen in a marathon gang bang. Adult Video News gave her the most enthusiastic review of her career:

> She's an active slut hound in this tape, taking on eight guys at once, sucking dick as though there were a penis famine in the Ladies' House of Corrections, allowing her body to be doused in champagne, then immolated with the searing heat of jizz. And you thought Savannah was a boring fuck.

Said Savannah: "I wanted to shock people, because I know people would never, ever, think that I would do anything like that. Next, I'm going to do my first anal."

In January 1994, Shannon made the cover of *Adult Video News*, and by spring, she was out of films, touring her strip act for $5,000 or more a week. Having kicked heroin, she'd managed to save $25,000 in cash. She started hanging out with Soleil Moon Frye, television's Punky Brewster. One day, Savannah led an expedition to a tattoo parlor. She had the "GREGG" on her right ankle changed into an angel.

At tax time, she had to pay $11,000 to the IRS. She bought

a $2,000 camcorder and $6,000 worth of dance costumes. She lent money to friends. She spent a lot on cocaine.

Then the money was gone.

Then the reverses began. She returned from a gig in New York with no paycheck; she'd spent all the money on a coke binge. Her next show was in early May, in Canada. The off-duty cop hired to bring her through customs gave her a choice: Lose the stash or remain in the States. She opted for the drugs. A few weeks later, in Pompano Beach, Florida, she got into a fistfight with her makeup man, Skip. They were dismissed. Again, no pay.

Savannah was becoming increasingly erratic. Where heroin helped her forget her problems, alcohol and cocaine made her crazy, stirred up the deep demons that had been so long on the nod. At a boxing match at the Forum that she attended with Danny Boy, Savannah punched a guy in the mouth after he called her "porno bitch." Another night, at a club with Julie—they'd made up, despite the outstanding loan—Savannah punched a guy and a brawl ensued. The girls were thrown out.

By now, Savannah was getting third notices from the landlord. She was depressed, but that was nothing new. She talked about killing herself, but that was nothing new either. "When the pressure gets too much, just push your finger here," she'd trill, making a gun with her thumb and forefinger, pointing to her temple.

"Just hold on," Nancy kept telling her. "You'll do the next gig and you'll have money again."

And so it was, on this Saturday night, July 9, a few days before she was due to fly to New York City to dance, that Savannah decided she needed some fun. Her friends all had plans. Her latest crush, Danny Boy, had left the country without telling her. Jason and his Hollywood homeboys would have to do.

"Well," said Jason to the assembled at Danny Boy's, "I guess we should roll."

"I need to take my dog home first," said Savannah. "Want to cruise with me, Jason?"

She had a really cool house, kind of *Miami Vice*, a little more hip, not cheesy. There were naked pictures of her everywhere, some of them six feet high. Jason was kind of on a shy tip, you know, looking but not looking. Savannah giggled at him. "You're so cute! You're blushing!" She stroked his cheek, then all of a sudden raised her shirt, proffered a boob. "I just had my second operation!" Jason was astounded.

Savannah proceeded to show him everything she owned. She pointed to every picture: "My boobs look pretty good here"; "That's when I shave for a film." She showed him her cats, Willie and Winnie, the place where her tropical-fish tank had been before the earthquake. She took him into her spare bedroom, devoted to dance costumes: her police uniform, her sailor uniform, her thigh-high spangled boots, her racks of boas and bras and G-strings.

She showed him her kitchen, her plates, her pots and pans, her refrigerator, her cupboards, filled with gourmet food from Williams-Sonoma, boxes of Kraft Macaroni and Cheese. She showed him her bedroom, her bathrooms, her view, her walk-through closet, her designer clothes and shoes and sunglasses and hats.

They landed in her living room, her black leather sofas, her glass coffee table. She poured wine and lit the dozens of candles set all around the room. She played deejay, poured wax over this plastic skull, poured wax on Jason's arm, just to fuck with him and stuff. It was cool. They were just laughing and hitting it off, exchanging gossip about stars and people they knew, just friendly, nothing sexual. They switched to some liquor that tasted like cinnamon.

At about four in the morning, Savannah stood up. "I wouldn't mind you sleeping over, but it's like our first night we've actually hung out," she said. "I don't think it would be a good idea. People get the wrong idea."

"That's cool," said Jason, forever amenable.

"I'll drive you home," said Savannah, giving him one more copy of *Sinderella*.

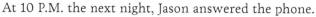

At 10 P.M. the next night, Jason answered the phone.

"Heeeloo-ooo, it's meee-eee!"

It was Sunday, club night for professionals like Jason, who left Saturdays to the weekend warriors. As was their custom, he and a few friends had pooled for a stretch limo. It beat the cost of DUIs.

Savannah arrived in a leather mini, black stockings, high heels, a skimpy top. Jason was like "Oh, my God! Shit!" She was drinking white wine straight from the bottle.

Club Renaissance was dead, so they went back to Danny Boy's and put on some tunes. Savannah talked a lot about Danny Boy. She also told Jason he was cool. "Some of the guys I go out with, you know, friends of people, they always try to get on me and stuff," she said. "It's cool that you're a gentleman. You don't treat me like a porno star."

At 12:30, Savannah suggested they go to her house. They took the Corvette. She drove like a maniac. Jason was screaming. Slow down! Slow down!

Boom! She hit the tree.

It was only a few hundred yards from her house, just around a curve. The Corvette was fucked. Pieces of the fence poked through the radiator. Steam rose into the starry night.

Savannah was freaking. They managed to drive the car up the hill, into her garage. Jason slammed his knee but was okay. Savannah had hit the windshield and the roof. They went to her bathroom. Blood and snot were running out of her nose, tears out of her eyes; it was really fucked up, the mascara leaving black streams, mingling with everything else, and she was hysterical. Her head was bleeding from the scalp. "Oh, God, oh, God, oh, God," she chanted, standing in from of her three-way mirror, dabbing at the blood with a washcloth. "I think my nose is broken," she said. She fainted, slid down the bathroom wall.

He threw some water in her face. She sputtered, woke up. Jason said he was going to call a doctor, but Savannah said no. She began to cry again. "My face! It's ruined! How am I going to do my show?"

"Come on," said Jason. "Get up. Why don't you take a Jacuzzi?"

Suddenly, Savannah popped up from the floor. "I have to call Nancy," she said, utterly composed. "Can you please go and take Daisy out and check the accident?"

When Jason returned, he couldn't find her. He went into the bathroom. The Jacuzzi was filling, bubbles rising. The candles were lit. Where was she? He went to the kitchen, then to the bedroom. He called out her names: "Shannon? Savannah?"

He walked through the closet, stuck his head out the doorway into the garage. She was sitting on the concrete floor, crying, rocking back and forth. "My car, my car is ruined," she moaned.

"Don't worry," said Jason. "You have insurance. You can get another one."

"But I was going to go look at Vipers with Danny Boy!"

Jason walked into the garage, knelt down, hugged her, kissed the top of her head, avoiding the blood. She didn't react.

"Listen," said Jason. "I'm gonna go turn off the Jacuzzi so it doesn't flood. I'll be right back, okay?"

Silence.

He came back, poked his head through the door. "Everything okay?"

Savannah looked up at him. "I'm so sorry," she said, and a tear rolled down her cheek, mingled with the blood. From behind her she pulled her blue steel .40-caliber semiautomatic Beretta.

She raised it to her head. When the pressure gets too much...

Bang!

Jason slammed the door shut, slumped back against it. His soft brown eyes were saucered with panic; his lightly muscled chest was pumping air. "She did not just do that," he groaned.

The rescue squad couldn't find the house; Nancy passed them on the way over, found Jason throwing up on the front lawn, went back down the hill and led them to Savannah. The exit wound looked like a tropical flower in her hair.

At 11 A.M., her dad ordered her life-support system unplugged. It was the first he'd seen her in four years. She took a last breath and died.

The expected ensued: "Death of a Porno Queen." The story had sex and drugs and rock and roll. The media scramble, and millions across America received a guilty teletronic kick in the thalamus, a shot of human urge. Nancy cooperated with everyone. "Savvy would have wanted a Marilyn Monroe funeral. Zillions of flowers, writing in the sky, lying in state at Forest Lawn."

Her father had her cremated. Savannah would have hated the tacky ceramic jar. He keeps it on a table in the living room, surrounded by pictures of his daughter.

Savannah's colleagues and acquaintances scrambled as well, for bragging rights and film rights, for status as best friend, biggest victim, most-wronged. Some indicted the industry, called for hot lines for troubled starlets. Many ducked for cover. Others said the industry was blameless, that Savannah's story was one of decline and fall, that there had never been a rise. The girl was doomed from conception, on a cool January night in Mission Viejo.

"DING DONG THE BITCH IS DEAD" was the headline in *Screw*. "Everyone knew that she was an airhead, and now she's got the hole in her dome to prove it," the item read. At the bottom of the page—which included a picture of Savannah with Xs drawn over her eyes—was a coupon to clip and mail: "I'm not brain-dead! I'll subscribe!"

Jason Swing told the police he was out walking Daisy when Savannah shot herself. He had lied, he says now, because he didn't want everyone saying he should have stopped her. What could he have done? Like, there was a blur, then a shot. When the media started blitzing, he found refuge in the offices of StormyLife Productions, working with producer Bruce Thabit and screenwriter Billy Milligan on the production of *Outside Eden*, a science-fiction action-thriller about a future encounter with aliens.

A superstar comes along only every three years or so in the porno industry. Tori Welles was the girl before Savannah. At 13, she gave a guy a blow job in exchange for a ride to Hollywood. By nightfall she had a pimp named T. He wore a hat.

Today, Tori Welles lives in a comfortable house in Topanga Canyon, with her two babies and a nanny. She has a nice Jewish husband, a former porn actor turned director. She commands $15,000 a week dancing in strip clubs across the country.

"You know," say Tori, "I get pissed off at these talk shows: 'Victim, victim, victim; abuse, abuse, abuse.' They use it to explain away everything. The real abuse comes when you let it rule your life. You just have to work through it. You have to help yourself however you can."

Sitting there on the garage floor, her nose broken, her car totaled, Shannon may have helped herself the only way she could. She acted ditsy, but she wasn't stupid. She was a porno queen; she earned her living having sex on film. That is what defined her, what her entire existence was about.

Shannon had no family and no past. No friends, no lover, no one who cared for her for purely unselfish reasons. Her life was in shambles; it had been that way from the very beginning. No doubt she thought it always would be.

When things got bad for Shannon, this was her usual reaction: curling into a ball, letting the events flood, waiting to see where she washed up.

Perhaps, on that warm July night, in a garage just over the hill from Hollywood, Shannon Wilsey committed the most willful act of her little life.

DEVIATES
IN LOVE

Swingers like to say that when you enter the door of the orgy room, you leave your clothes and your labels behind you. Welcome to the Elite International Couples' Fantasy weekend in Pensacola, Florida, where anyone can be a swan.

Finally there's a knock at the door, and Walter drains his glass, sets it on the night table. A candle flickers in the dark; lurid shadows dance across two double beds in room 416 of the Sunset Lodge. Walter breathes into his hand and sniffs. *Well*, he thinks, *here goes anything.*

He drops his palms to his thighs and stands, grunting a bit, that noise a man makes when the files of personal history have begun to pile up around him, action resigned but not quite resolved. He looks down at Debbie. "You're sure now, right?"

Debbie watches the candle, a vaguely musky number from the knick-knack store in the mall. Tiny creases score her lips, the corners of her mouth, yet she has about her a gleam of trust and wonderment. She likes her drinks, usually fruit juice and vodka, with a straw. When she's done, she'll root around in the ice, search out the last little sip, make a loud sucking noise until someone gets irritated. Then she'll giggle, take one last sip.

"We can always say no," Walter says. "I mean—"

"Just open the door already, Walter. You're thinking too much again, remember?"

Thinking. Walter has realized lately that there's too much thinking in his life. He's found that once he starts thinking, a program of pros and cons starts to run. He compares, contrasts, weighs, frets. He replays his failures, sets up his odds. His mind begins to build traps, reasons not to do things. The night before they flew to Pensacola, Walter was in bed, covers up to his chin, trying to imagine what lay in store. A cold drop of sweat rolled across his rib cage. He reached for the phone, asked Deb, "Do you think we're being crazy?"

Walter was more than a little apprehensive about being with people who really had a lot of experience, who really had an open lifestyle. If he wanted, he could count on three fingers the number of lovers he'd had since 1977. Even he and Deb had never done it. They'd gotten naked one night and talked about AIDS. Then they fell asleep.

Now Walter takes a deep breath, thumbs his shin into his waistband, walks briskly to the door.

"Right on time!" he sings.

"Howdy!" chorus Ann and Michael.

Ann is wearing something like a wedding dress, white and lacy, see-through: garter belt, G-string, bustier, veil. Michael is wearing a policeman's uniform. Instead of a nightstick, he carries a two-foot marital aide. Flesh-colored, veined, and rubbery, it has heads at either end.

Walter looks at Debbie. Debbie looks at Walter. Nobody told them anything about costumes.

Down the hall is room 425, the hospitality suite for the Elite International Couples' Fantasy weekend. As soon as the deejay had put on the last record and announced, "Ladies and gentlemen, lets go party," a good many of the fifty couples registered had come straight here. At the moment, a number of them are arranged into a daisy chain. Its origin is way over there, two women on the king-size bed. It flows across the patterned spread, head to pelvis, pelvis to head, down over the carpet, a long train coupled orally, tresses and pates, arms and legs, mouths and breasts, writhing and flexing, diddling and bobbing, past the table of mixers and munchies, around a corner and through the sitting room, past a flickering video orgy, past the sofa, a red-haired man masturbating, his eyes wide and unfocused, past a woman in a gold lame dress sleeping in a fetal position against the wall, on through the open door and into the hallway.

They are a wide assortment, people you wouldn't second-glance, ages thirty to sixty, from towns and cities from Florida to Michigan, Virginia to Arkansas. Mothers, fathers, grandparents. A horse trainer, a housewife, a state trooper, a minister, an owner of a travel agency, an executive secretary, a psychologist, a man high up in the music industry, a real estate agent, a salesman for a satellite dish company, a computer operator, a truck driver, a mail-order clerk, an employee of Oscar Mayer. Of course, what they do, where they live, none of that matters here. People in swinging like to say that when you enter the door of the orgy room, you leave your clothes and your labels behind you. You step out of your bikini briefs or your cutout bra and into a world of anonymity, a moist, dark place where your fantasies can be real.

Here, as one woman says in her personal ad in *Heartland Swingers* magazine, you can be a Horny Housewife from western Michigan, 5'4", 140 lbs, 38D, brown hair and *eyes* and shaved, very bi. Or a Voluptuous Nympho (39–22–34) into tight spread-wide-open bondage, spanking, nothing too outrageous or kinky. Or an Attractive, Rubenesque White Female; a Well-hung (9") Tom Selleck Look-alike; an Open-minded Couple looking for romance, variety, and good times.

In room 425, men and women traipse around nakedly in their alter egos, regular folks from real closet mirrors, toupees and wrinkles and bellies and stretch marks, cellulite and black socks, tiptoeing over limbs and bodies, dipping chips, taking pictures with Instamatics. A couple stands outside on the balmy lanai, watching the go-cart races at the grand-prix track across the parking lot. Inside, a platinum blonde rides something that looks like a Naugahyde saddle. Attached to the seat, facing skyward, *is* a plastic phallus. The device can be set for rotation, vibration, or both. The record ride is five minutes. The blonde, dismounting after three, stays down on one knee, clasps her hands. "Will you marry me?" she asks the machine.

Cruising around the room, a fully dressed man shoulders a video camera. In a month or so, hundreds or even thousands of Americans will own a copy of the action this evening, courtesy of A'Mature Video Productions. For fifteen dollars they will be able to pop the video into their living-room VCRs and—after a brief warning about the content, a guarantee of the amateur status of the consenting players, and a short, poignant message about the need for political involvement on behalf of the First Amendment—the action will unfold on a room full of people in various states of undress, some wearing feathered bird masks, or capes, or leopard-skin bras, the floor littered with boas and toy cat-o'-nine tails and ripped-open foil condom packets, the accompanying soundtrack a symphony of moans and slurps and sucking sounds, the intimate, primal music of nighttime, heartfelt and abandoned, stirringly grotesque, Oh, God! Fuck me.' Come on, baby!

Up and down the hall, meanwhile, twosomes and threesomes and foursomes and more pursue every conceivable conjunction, employ every lotion and toy. And, at this very moment, all across America, millions of others are doing the same. Here in the 1990s, the age of AIDS, the era of guilt and caution and remorse, a directory of swing clubs across the nation lists almost one hundred. These are the big fancy places, with theme rooms and exhibition rooms and even rooms for the night. Uncounted hundreds, maybe even thousands, are less formal, convening weekly in private homes for a door fee. Al and April,* the hosts this weekend in Pensacola, have more than one hundred couples that meet twice monthly in Nashville as the Tennessee Social Club. One of their employees heads up Personal Touch, a group of sixty couples meeting on alternate weekends. Add these to one other swing club in Nashville, home of both the Baptists' and the Methodists' national Sunday-school boards. Recently, a negative article in a local paper brought twenty-six new members to Al s club alone.

Al also sells annually more than half a million copies of swingers' magazines in all fifty states. There are dozens of other magazines like his, each one containing hundreds of personal appeals from singles and couples. Some couples only trade photos or videos. Others exchange first names and then body fluids. Variety, fantasy fulfillment, a hobby shared by man and wife, that is the notion. Shaving, Greek, Roman, gang bangs, girls' nights, light S and M, or maybe even romance—dinner, dancing, and sex. Husbands who want to see their wives with other women. Wives who want to see their husbands with other women. Husbands who want to see their wives with other men while they take pictures. Wives who want to be with several men while their husbands take pictures. Cross-dressing, sexy lingerie, Mistress Missy looking for a sex slave, no male bisexuality, please.

Until tonight, Walter's life had basically gone all wrong. He'd given up music to get married and raise a family. The day after his daughter was born, his wife was diagnosed with schizophrenia. Imagine the worst and that's the rest. Business reverses, legal problems, heartbreaks, hassles, years. Now Walter is forty-four, an optometrist with a renovated condo in a Victorian building in Cleveland. He works part-time, makes his money trading commodities. Through the years he's been into Nautilus, biking, liquid diets, rowing, jogging. A series of memberships at video stores has left him an expert in the history of film; a series of lackluster weekends has left him a master of Trivial Pursuit. One day about two months ago, he daydreamed about hanging himself from the chin-up bar in the ten-foot doorway to his den. He could see the last spastic jerk of his feet. He was wearing his Nikes.

Now, with all the hope and spirit he can muster—with enough presence of mind to know that his life isn't yet over, that you can find more but only *if* you seek—he is sitting on a bed across from an erotic bride and her Village People police escort in a cut-rate motel room in Pensacola, Florida. Next to him on the bed is his good friend Debbie. She was married for twelve years, has two kids. Recently, her husband married her best friend.

"Well," says Michael, "you all aren't soft swingers, are you?"

"What's a soft swinger?" asks Walter, crunching a piece of *ice.*

"Soft swingers go along with everything right up until sex, and then they don't have sex," says Michael. The words seem to leave a bad taste in his mouth. Ann raises an eyebrow.

"That doesn't sound like me at all," says Walter. "I kinda want to get right into it."

"Enthusiastic, ain't he!" laughs Michael. Ann and Walter and Debbie laugh, too. Michael puts his hand on Ann's knee, just below a colorful tattoo of a bird of paradise. Ann smiles, catches her husband's gaze. It is a fond and loving exchange, twenty-three years of marriage, but also somehow carnal and new, sparks of lust and devilment dancing in the humid, salty air of the Gulf night. They hold it there a moment, and then Ann breaks off and turns her head slowly, seeking Walter.

Fairly attractive, Walter *is* thinking. *Not bad at all. Blond hair, always nice, and a very nice shape.* He wonders what he could see *if* she uncrossed her legs. Her breasts seem nice, not real large but swelling ever so slightly above her bustier. And very soft skin, so white. He wonders, *Should I do something? What should I say? I guess I could—*

Ann reaches out across the space between the beds, long black fingernails...

"When I married him," Ann is saying, "I didn't know nothing."

"The first time I went down on her, she like to had a heart attack!" says Michael.

"I'd never had it done," protests Ann, giggling. "I was really, really dumb on it.

I created a monster now," says Michael.

"I was basically a very shy person," says Ann.

Michael double-takes, smiles. "We'd heard of swinging on TV."

"He just asked me to try it," says Ann. "He said, 'If you try it and you don't like it, I'll never ask you again.' "

"Cause I never forced her into nothing."

"I'm a person, if I don't want to do something, I won't."

"Yeah," says Michael.

"You start talking around, and you find out there's a lot of people out there in the lifestyle. We met some of them, then we put an ad in a swinger magazine."

"They'd call and then we'd meet at the Waffle House or something. You never knew what you'd be getting into. One couple, the guy had just had two open-heart surgeries within three or four months," says Ann.

"And he didn't have a dick on him," says Michael. "He had an artificial dick. A good piece of pussy and a glass of ice water woulda killed him."

"Oh, Michael," says Ann, "be kind."

Michael smiles. "I like to see her with a guy that's a lot bigger than me. It just turns me on. There's just something there that gets to me. I think I'd also like her to be with another woman. She's never been with another woman. She's curious, though."

"I am curious," says Ann. "You could say I just like a lot of sex."

"That's what it boils down to," says Michael. "Excitement."

An hour or so past dawn, the sun edges between the curtains, rays of a new day filtering across rumpled clothes and scattered bed sheets, a smell of ashtrays, old beer, perspiration. Walter feels himself swimming slowly upward from deep, pleasant dreams. Michael and Ann had left several hours earlier, happy and holding hands, walking naked together down the hall to their own room. Now Walter dozes in the grainy silken waters just beneath awake. He stretches, rolls over onto his back, luxuriates beneath the sheets. He notices something, a certain morning tightness down there that he hasn't felt in quite a while. He clasps his hands behind his head, breathes deeply. He thinks of Ann, last night. He smiles.

It was he who got things started. Not very long after Ann had taken to edging her black fingernails along his knee, Walter stood up, pulled off his shirt, went for her. Michael, following, had gone for Deb. Walter took Ann's face lightly between his hands, gave her a deep kiss. They flopped on the bed.

More kissing, undressing, some hugging, and then Ann took the lead and dropped her head. They stayed like this until Walter started feeling guilty, so he found a way to kind of flip her over. They spent maybe fifteen or twenty minutes there, and then came a time when he and Ann reached a silent decision, well, okay, now let's go for regular. From above Ann, he could see Michael and Debbie, and as he labored, every once in a while he would reach over and touch Deb and give her a little massage, just to let her know he was there.

After a while, Walter noticed that Ann was starting her orgasm. He was glad she was first. All the pressure to please and perform was off his back. Her body tightened beneath him, her breathing became quicker and then shallower and shallower and then caught, and then there was nothing for a moment, a pause, a strained, constricted calm, a trembling, a teetering on the edge, and then a sudden eruption of breath and voice and movement, and that gave Walter the clue to go ahead and get his. He looked over toward Michael and Debbie, and he could see that Michael's movements were almost identical to his own, a counter beat, a split second behind. Walter could feel a rising synchronicity or something in the room, a multiplication of emotions, a rush of sounds and energy like a choral round. First silence, then the first voice, and then the second, and a resonance begins to build, a fullness, new harmonics and vibrations born neither of the first nor the second, but rather of the mixing of both, all of it welling up, filling the room. Walter flashed for an instant on his days with transcendental meditation. *Om mani padme om*, the jewel is in the lotus. Walter was 100 percent into it. No mind games, no cares, totally immersed.

Now Debbie stirs in the morning light, and Walter opens his eyes, looks across the white sheets at her tangle of brown curls. Debbie purrs, scoots up close, her lips near his ear. "Walter," she whispers, singing like a little girl, "*Waaalter!*"

"Yes, Deb?"

"I still feel sexy."

"You do, do you?"

"Yes," she says, and then she giggles and ducks her head beneath the sheet.

"Smile, honey.'" calls Al, trundling barefoot through deep sand, the camcorder riding his shoulder, appended to one eye. He moves in, fingers a button on the handle. A thick black lens telescopes, a tight electric whine. Close-up on April.

"Say *orgasm.¹*" directs Al. April lifts her head, squints into the brilliant day. She smiles wanly, raises the middle finger of her right hand.

"Fuck you very much, sweetheart," sings Al. He is forty-six, a bit of the handsome goofball, a bit of the Artful Dodger, a homespun cottonseed from Arkansas. He has a full head of gray hair combed back into a postmodern pompadour, squared-off aviator bifocals, cleft chin, eight-inch penis. And he has trouble. April. Here on the weekend that they've gathered fifty couples in Pensacola, there's a crisis. Yesterday, they had sex only twice. They seem to be breaking up.

It's a Pygmalion-and-Galatea-type story, Henry Higgins and Eliza Doolittle. Al's scared, a little desperate. She, on the other hand, *is* firm but ambivalent, in control of her facts and her future but not of her emotions. She knows she needs to take what she's learned and fly. Yet she feels like she owes him so much. Sitting on the beach with Al, she'll dangle her foot near him on the sand, tickle his thigh with her toes. He'll be so hopeful at the sign that he'll rare up and go for a hug, then push it, try to get sexy. She'll push it away. That's not what she meant.

"Have a *niiiiiice day*, dear," calls Al, and he turns and heads down the beach, preceded by his lens. His belly bobbles but not too bad, minimal damage considering he gave up jogging five years ago.

Now he comes to a stop, pans the scenery around him. The cloudless sky, the greens and blues of the warm, salty Gulf

of Mexico, the fine white sand, an assortment of string biki-
nis, seashell-cup bras, mottled thighs, hairy bellies, motel towels,
and rented chaise longues, the swingers from Elite. One group
is huddled around the travel agent and his wife. They have a
binder of photos and brochures from swing clubs and nudist
hotels they've visited across the world. Out in the water, a man
and a woman play catch with a second man's bathing suit. The
naked guy bobs whitely in the chest-high waves, hands raised in
resignation.

"Sharks!" yells Al. "Watch out for your dick.'"

April checks the water. "That shark's gonna go hungry."

Al stays focused on the water, hoping the naked guy will
make a break for it.

He's lovable, Al is, a little irritating but willing to play the fall guy,
an off-color comedian who's a tad too loud. He grew up in an
orphanage, studied psychology in college, served in Vietnam. His
life's work has been sales: insurance, solar power, real estate, and,
for the last ten years, the swinging lifestyle. He's been swinging for twenty years, been married twice, says he's had more
than three thousand women. In the chiropractor's office, under
Frequency of Intercourse, he recently wrote "four to five daily."

Al twists around, shooting down the beach toward the
fishing pier, and then around a little more, moving in a tight
circle, panning the dunes, the highway, the hotel . . . There.'
Coming down the boardwalk from the pool. He fingers the zoom.
He whistles. "The Star-Spangled Banner!" he yells. "Hot damn!"

Butch and Rosemary step in tandem off the last wooden
plank. Simultaneously, each kicks off one rubber thong, then the
other, then bends, grabs, straightens up. Butch and Rosemary
have been going to the beach together for twenty-one years.
He carries the cooler, she totes the bag of stuff. He's tall, very
thin, slightly bow-legged (a souvenir of his rodeo days), wearing a gimme cap over his toupee. A ponytail, one inch long,
secured with a red rubber band, pokes out beneath the plastic
adjuster. Rosemary is forty but has a gym in her house. When

she appeared last night at the costume party in that tiny black thing, you could see men all over the room poking their wives in the rib cage. Quite a few wives poked back. This afternoon she's wearing a very small bathing suit. The top is blue with two white stars. The bottom is a patch of stripes.

"I don't know whether to salute you or stand at attention!" exclaims Al.

"Looks like you're already standing at attention " says Butch.

"You know it's you I want, Butchie," says Al, reaching with his free hand toward Butch's bathing suit. Butch jumps back. Everybody laughs.

"Al! Enough!" pleads April.

April met Al at a swingers' party four years ago. She was forty-five pounds heavier then, recently separated, two young kids, still the same ugly duckling at twenty-six that she had been ten years earlier when she'd played Monopoly with her parents on the night of her senior prom. Since teaming up with Al, she said recently in a speech to their swing club, she has grown into a swan.

Indeed, the combination of April's business ideas and Al's salesmanship has built for the couple a modest empire based on swinging. From the looks of his station wagon, a rusted woody with two hundred thousand miles on the odometer, and the number of alimony and child-support checks he writes each month, they haven't amassed a fortune. But they have taken over a warehouse in Nashville, and the payroll has grown to fourteen people. Somehow, Al and April have managed to tap a well of latent desire in America. If the exponential growth of their own mailing list is any indication, the well *is* deep.

In addition to the adult-contact magazines—fifty state and regional, five national—Al and April also run a set of 900-numbers with twenty-four-hour operators who can connect interested swingers; another set of 900-numbers with revolving date lines and recordings; the Preferred Lovers toy collection; the Tennessee Social Club, meeting twice monthly in the Free

Spirit Lounge, a bar in the rear of their warehouse; the Elite International Paradise weekends in Hot Springs, Las Vegas, on a Mississippi riverboat. As Am-World Distributors, they produce A'Mature, Fantasy Focus, and Real Swingers Videos, offering a catalogue of ninety-two home-porn videos. All of the videos star everyday people, and many of them were made with this very same Sears camcorder. Many of them feature April, in her guise as Mary Lou.

"Mary Lou" is one of the brightest new lights in the fast-emerging field of amateur porn. Recently, her picture was on the cover of *Hustler's Amateur Video guide*. She is famous for her high cheekbones, her inch-long nipples, her wanton enthusiasm, and her hard, jockey-style rides on prone partners. In *Mary Lou, the Stud Finder*, a woman hires a carpenter "with all the right equipment." *Missy, Mary Lou, and 9 Inches* has April teaming up with a housewife from Arkansas.

The video line was April's idea, though it started out before they met as one of Al's grand schemes. At first, he wanted to make professional-quality movies with amateur actors, people that the folks at home could identify with. He himself had always enjoyed watching and taking pictures. And though the women he'd swung with weren't goddesses or even of professional porn quality, they were willing, enthusiastic, and accessible. The same was true of the men. Swinging had held a considerable amount of his attention for twenty years, why not the buying public?

When April came on board, she took the idea and ran. She nixed the professional sound and video men Al had hired, bought the video camera, and threw it in the back of the wagon. Three years later, Al and April are selling about ten thousand videos annually, many of them starring their friends, some of them sent unsolicited from the heartland, all of them featuring real people having real sex, the good, the bad, the ugly.

According to the video industry, porn films account for 12 percent of all national rentals, about $325 million a year. Currently, amateur videos are the hottest new trend, written up in the *New York Times,* debated on *Donahue,* available at your corner store. About a dozen companies offer amateur videos of one sort or another, from homemade to professional.

It is impossible to say how big the market is, but the reasons for its popularity are apparent to Al and April and everyone else here in Pensacola. Like swinging, the videos aren't as much about fantasy as they are about fulfillment. You can dream about Traci Lords or John Holmes, but you can drive to Pensacola and fuck a half-dozen real men or women in one day even if you have stretch marks or a little dick. Amateur videos make everything seem possible. The stars resemble you and your neighbors, and they're not embarrassed. It looks like they're having a pretty great time, all the grunting and the straining, the unrelenting pleasure, all of it real and unrehearsed. Swingers think of it like this: Sex is the one recreation that God gave us. It costs nothing. It requires no accessories. You can even do it alone. It is a natural drug available in an almost inexhaustible supply. The Chinese, the Greeks, the Romans, the Hindus, the Buddhists, all of them believed in variety. It was only with the rise of Western civilization that sex lost all its glamour. Done among consenting adults with proper respect for health, it feels good, it is good, can even have lasting benefits. Why not make it a hobby?

All of which sounded ridiculous to April the first time she heard it. She'd grown up in a traditional upper-middle-class family in the Baptist South. Mother, father, sister, dog, cat, tropical fish. When she was twelve years old, she fell head over heels in love. He was two years older. In truth, the boy kind of dated April when he didn't have anybody else. But April had read enough Harlequin romances to believe that if you stick around long enough, eventually they fall in love with you. In his last year of high school, the boy got another girl pregnant. They were married. April went away to college.

Two years later April herself was married, to a man she'd met while working part-time at a hospital. After a few minutes of conversation, he told her, "I'm gonna marry you," and April said, "Oh, sure, right." A week later he said it again, and April thought, *Well, it would certainly be one way to get out of moving back home.* He was twenty years older, built nursing homes. They lived in a seven-foot travel trailer.

Seven years and two kids later, April got a phone call one day from her original love. The next weekend she and the two kids moved to Nashville.

And so it was, deep into her fourth week in Nashville, that the boyfriend suggested swinging, and April went along. She'd never heard of swinging. He didn't explain. The party was at a private house.

At first, April didn't see anything out of order. She had a drink, talked a while. After about fifteen minutes, she went downstairs.

It was the most disgusting thing she had ever seen. She didn't even tell him she was leaving. She took the car.

For some reason, she doesn't know why, April agreed to a second party in Memphis two weeks later, and there she met Al. For the next six weeks, Al and April saw a lot of each other. They'd go to lunch, to dinner, to the park, on walks. April started thinking, *What have I done wrong? This guy's got a reputation for fucking everything and he isn't even making passes.*

Finally, Al explained. He wanted more from April than a swinging relationship. Soon they moved in together, though they didn't begin swinging for nine months. He just said when you're ready, you're ready. She knows now that if you try to talk a woman into swinging, she's not going to last very long.

April can't remember her first time swinging as a couple with Al, but she remembers clearly something she calls "my first real assertion of who I was sexually."

It was in Nashville, maybe a year into swinging. She and Al were giving a party at a hotel. Usually, they didn't do a lot at their own parties, too many details and responsibilities. But this time, there was a man from Kentucky she'd been trying to get with for six months. She took his hand, led him out of the dance. On the way to the elevator, she bumped into another man she knew. "Where you guys going?" he asked. "Come on," said April. In the elevator were others. They followed, too.

Later, Al came upstairs and peeked into the room. April was with six men. He stood in the doorway for a long, long time, smiling, shaking his head. His swan.

April lost weight, discovered the mall, started wearing makeup and going to the beauty shop each week, changing her hair color several times a year. She moved into the business, engineered the deal for the warehouse, took the big office for herself, decorated it in dusky rose. Currently, she has ads under twenty-five different names running in personals magazines all over the country. She also has a mini-industry in Mary Lou—900-numbers, videos, photo sales, fans.

"If you've had a traditional upbringing, and you listen to society, it's difficult to think of giving somebody you care about to somebody else. But Al says that our swinging relationships are part of our lovemaking. He says that swinging is like using a living dildo, and to a certain extent it *is*—it's our toys, our foreplay. We always go home and do it together, and that's always the best, though I have to say being with others helps a lot.

"I don't know if you get technically better at sex 'cause you're in the lifestyle, but I think you're a little more experimental. You're a little less embarrassed because in a lot of cases you really don't know the person that well. To me, the most embarrassing moment is taking off your clothes. After that, it's all spontaneous. You just turn off your mind and hook up your nerve endings.

"It's like the movies. I've had a few offers to do it professionally, and it's like, no, 'cause you guys would screw it all up. You'd say be here at 8:00, you're gonna do tit shots at 9:00, and this at 10:00. No way! That takes all the fun out of it.

"I have to say, getting letters from people who want pictures of my feet, who send me forty dollars for them, well, how can that not be good for you? You don't want to meet the guys, but listen: There's men out there jerking off to me. That gives you a certain amount of confidence.

"Lately, I've been noticing that my insecurities are going away. I'm really starting to feel good about myself. It's the wallflower stuff. I mean, it used to be that everything was unobtainable. Now I decide. Hell, now I turn it down in droves.'"

By late Saturday afternoon, the sun has dipped, fat and orange, below the water slide at Tiki Island. Birds fly, crickets chirp, waves tongue the shoreline. The water is calm and evanescent, the color of jewels, animated in the autumn light, a Disney sea. It is time now for the cookout, and everyone is here by the pool—even the state trooper, who has been known in the past to take a cooler full of sandwiches into the orgy room and stay there the entire weekend. Rosemary undulates on high heels across the grass, a heaping plate in one hand, an iced tea sloshing in the other. Her corn-silk hair floats on the breeze, her white spandex mini rides high on her thighs. Butch, her husband, trails a few steps behind.

Rosemary pulls up beside one of the picnic tables. "Mind if we sit down?" she sings, and then she nods backward, indicating Butch. "I already heard everything this one's got to say at least three times."

Michael and Ann, Walter and Deb, Sarah, Teresa, and Rod erupt in a chorus of laughter and commiseration. Swinging, especially a weekend gathering like this, is about social foreplay—the banter, the romance, the chase, the newness of a stranger's old stories. It's like having a quick affair, only your spouse is doing the same, often in the same room. Everyone shifts around on the benches to make room. A spot opens opposite Walter.

Holy shit! he thinks, and some saliva actually puddles in his mouth. He swallows, feels a slight blush. God! Walter had somehow missed Rosemary at the party last night. Today, he and Debbie and Michael and Ann had gone to a nude beach near the Naval Air Station. They had a nice day, walking, talking, having sex two different times. Deb and Michael really had a connection going. They couldn't keep their hands off each other. This was fine with Walter. He hadn't gotten laid this much since... he'd never gotten laid this much. Michael and Ann had kind of indicated that they really wanted to be with only one other couple for the weekend. That's the way they usually go, and that was fine with Walter. Until now.

"What y'all talking about?" asks Rosemary.

"That Professor Hill woman," says Sarah.

"It's on every channel," exclaims Deb.

As it happens, this weekend, the Hon. Clarence Thomas is undergoing a contentious nomination hearing for a seat on the Supreme Court of the United States. At the center of the public's interest in the televised proceedings are sexual harassment allegations leveled against Thomas by Anita Hill, a law professor who had previously worked under Thomas.

According to Hill, Thomas spoke to her of acts that he had seen in pornographic films, including women having sex with animals, group sex and, rape scenes. Most remembered would be this tidbit, after they had both taken new jobs at the EEOC: "Thomas was drinking a Coke in his office, he got up from the table at which we were working, went over to his desk to get the Coke, looked at the can and asked, 'Who has put pubic hair on my Coke?'"

"It's getting to the point where a man can't tell a woman she has a nice ass," says Michael.

"Or nice tits," adds Rod.

The women around the table chew quietly. *Men, whattaya gonna do?* Butch is quiet, too. *This is gonna be interesting,* he thinks.

"I still think she made the whole thing up," says Michael.

"What about you, Rosemary? What do you think?" It is Walter. He smiles, sweetly.

"What do I think?" asks Rosemary, licking some sauce off a finger. She looks across at Butch. He finds something very interesting in his plate. "Well," says Rosemary. "Men aren't fast enough on their feet to figure out when they're fuckin' up. Or maybe they don't give a shit. One or the other."

Then she stands, tugs at her mini. She says, bright and perky, "I'm gettin' me another piece of chicken! You want anything, Butch, honey? Any, y'all?"

She turns on her toes, moves away toward the barbecue pit.

Walter watches keenly. He wants her. Now.

"I was raised very religious, a Jehovah's Witness," says Rosemary. "I was dressed from here to here my whole life. My first husband was even against oral sex. Then I met this one and about three years into our relationship he said, 'Let's go to a swingers' party.' "

"I suggested it because ever since I was, I don't know, fourteen years old, one woman's never satisfied me," says Butch.

"No," interrupts Rosemary. "You just like to see two women together."

"You damn straight I do.'"

"Well, darlin', I've lived with you eight years and we've had three single women and four couples, so obviously those eight years and those seven experiences don't tell me that you haven't been satisfied with just me."

"Yeah, could be."

"Thank you," says Rosemary. "When he first suggested swinging, I was curious as to what the hell went on. The thing people say about Jehovah's Witnesses is that they go to church and roll under the chairs and try to find God. I guess that brought a lot of people out to see exactly what they did do on Sundays. And I was the same way about the swingers club, wanting to know what happened.

"First we went through a phase of single women only. I have to tell you, I had my doubts. But with the right female it's very enjoyable. I've had some women who could eat pussy a lot better then men ever thought they could. I've gotten to the point where I've had to push them away 'cause I didn't want anybody in that room to see what I was going through.

"Then we went through a phase of women with their husbands, but we didn't swap, there was no total swapping. Then we tried the actual swap situation. It got to the point where a lot of the women were as attractive to me as they were to Butch, but

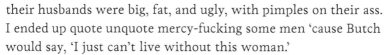

their husbands were big, fat, and ugly, with pimples on their ass. I ended up quote unquote mercy-fucking some men 'cause Butch would say, 'I just can't live without this woman.'

"But then it got to the point that I said, 'Wait a minute, this ain't gonna work for me no more. For once I want it the way I want it even if you gotta fuck a dog.' And he said, 'Well, I can't get my dick up, but you can use lubricant.' But now, finally, it's taken us four years, but now he'll say, 'What do you think of the blonde's husband over there?' You've got to work through the games. If you don't, divorce *will* ensue. What's good for the goose is good for the gander.

"And I'll tell you another thing," says Rosemary. "If cleanliness isn't next to you, neither are we. One thing that turns us off is couples that *will* not use condoms. I realize that the guys don't get the same damn sensation, but tough luck. Hell, no dick's worth dying for."

"There's a shitload of men, and women too, that will tell you they never look at anybody else," says Butch. "Well, that's bullshit. If she tells me she'll never go to bed with another man, and then she does it behind my back and I find out, then she has lied to me. If she lies to me about that, then she'll lie to me about anything. I'll begin to get where I don't trust her with the money we make or with my truck or with anything.

"Then you get into deceit and lies and mistrust and all this other bullshit. What it comes down to is that if you can trust your wife to go to bed with somebody else and be honest about it, you can trust her about anything."

"Good evening. How *is* everybody feeling? Good-looking crowd here tonight. A bunch of dancin' fools!" announces Steve the deejay, breaking the music, turning up the patter. He drags on his cigarette, blows the smoke into the microphone: *whooosh*. Once upon a time, he was a stand-up comic.

Steve squints down from his platform, into the candle-lit hall. "Apparently, some of our guests didn't figure out that the costume party was last night. I see Butch came dressed as a bald guy. Where's your toupee, Butch? Oh, yeah, didn't I run over something hairy on the go-cart track? I thought it was road kill."

"I wiped your ass on the go-cart track." hollers Butch.

"Shoot," says Steve. "Well, anyway... Butch, you doin' okay this weekend?"

"Had five offers so far!"

"If you keep on, maybe a *woman* will offer before the night's over! Ha-ha! *Whooosh*... We're gonna keep it pumped up right now. This guy can sing his ass off when it comes to love songs..."

The music starts and the dance floor fills. Some do a western two-step, working in a circle around the floor; others attempt white disco. A few couples slow dance, unconcerned with the beat. Hands move inside shirts, under skirts. At the tables, people talk and flirt. Deb, it seems, has discovered Gary. Michael and Ann have found Keith and BJ.

Al is at the back of the room, behind a partition, sulking, losing himself in the task of taking pictures of each couple, a Polaroid for them, real film for the article in the swingers' magazines. April has taken to champagne. She stopped drinking four years ago, but tonight she's bought the good stuff with the flowers painted on the bottle. She's been hovering around Rosemary, spilling bubbles on the rug, and also around Steve's girl, Shannon. Shannon is a looker, too. She partied for the first time last night, choosing Butch and Rosemary for her inaugural. To Rosemary it was a mercy fuck, but she liked Shannon, wanted to do it for her and Butch. Afterward, Shannon and Steve went back to their own room and did it until dawn. Shannon came to breakfast droopy-eyed and flushed. "Eleven times," she kept repeating. By lunch they were engaged.

Walter, meanwhile, is sitting at a table by himself. He's in a certain odd frame of mind. Since dinner he's been looking around. He's kind of decided that there are certain people he wants to be with. Really wants to be with. There is Rosemary, of course. A girl of his dreams. If she'd only ask, he'd go at it right now on the floor next to his chair. Shannon is another. He'd do her in a minute. Why won't she come over?

Walter's mind is beginning to play its old tricks on him. His mind is saying, *You really want to have sex with all of these women.* His mind is building a trap for him. *Expectations.* It's saying, *You have a huge appetite and you're not going to satisfy it.*

Walter is depressed. Actually depressed. His palms hold the sides of his head. There is more on my plate in front of me than I can possibly have, he is thinking. Things aren't turning out as I'd imagined. For some reason, I thought women might be more aggressive during this thing. But they aren't. I thought they'd just come up and say, "Hey, let's do something." That is basically how it had been with Michael and Ann. But that was eons ago, twenty-four hours. Why isn't Rosemary asking me to dance? he wonders. Why not Shannon? Why aren't they dragging me to their rooms?

Suddenly Walter feels a tap on his back. He twists around, hopeful, smiling his best smile.

Her eyebrows are drawn in with pencil. Through her filmy top he can see sad little pancake breasts. She has to be sixty. "Would you like to dance?" she asks.

A lone silhouette against the night horizon, Walter stands on the beach, arms crossed over his fishnet shirt, feet planted up to his ankles in the sand, head thrown back, the view of infinity. *A million stars,* he thinks. This is what they mean by a million stars. Funny about nature, about beauty, pleasure, love: Things so strong and deep and lovely and mysterious become cliches when you try to form the words, try to tell yourself what you see or feel. A million stars. A gentle wind. The smell of salt, the sound of waves, the cool, gritty tickle of sand between your toes. *Stop telling yourself where you are,* Walter chides himself. *Just be here.*

Walter is none too happy. The party had ended and Debbie had gone off in search of Gary, and Walter found himself sitting at the table, lights out, alone. He went to his room a while, watched TV, sulked. He kept thinking about Rosemary. He wondered who she was with. He imagined being with her. He masturbated. He felt jealous, cheated, confirmed in his opinion that his life had been one big waste of time, a period he was damned to endure.

Now, standing on the beach, his burden slowly begins to lift; he begins to see things in a slightly different way. There is something about a view like this, the infinity. Your disappointments have a distance to travel before falling back down to pierce your hopes. They lift off, rocket out and away. Back on the ground the smoke clears, and you can see new things. Walter realizes that he was so paralyzed by the weight of choice, the chance of rejection, that he never made any move at all. So much in his life had been that way. He fucked himself up once and he never trusted himself again, never even gave himself a break. Now here he is. He'd tried something new, sort of. For a day at least, he tried something new and it had made him happy. Then he got too happy. Then he got scared. Then he got sad.

My expectations were way up there, he tells himself, kind of up where the stars are. What was I thinking? What did I want? What more? Come on. I really did have a good time. I had a fabulous time. This isn't an athletic event. I really had a lot of wonderful things happen. Let's face it—if nothing else happens during the whole trip, it was still miraculous. If I die in an accident right now, I can go out with a smile on my face.

Walter closes his eyes, feeling the cool air on his nipples through the mesh of his shirt, the growing lightness in his heart. He stands awhile, stock-still, breathing in and out, trying not to think, trying just to feel.

"Howdy, stranger. What are you doin' out here all by your lonesome?"

Walter turns, slowly, not wanting to believe. It is Rosemary. Her white miniskirt glows in the starlight.

"Hi," he says.

"Hi."

"Ah, where's Butch?"

"Oh, you know Butch. Gettin' into one thing or another."

"If I had you, I wouldn't need anyone else," says Walter.

"That's sweet," says Rosemary, avoiding his eyes. She looks up, sighs. Walter does the same. "How beautiful," she says.

"A million stars," says Walter.

"A million stars."

They are silent awhile, facing each other, heads back, gazing up. Then Walter's head comes down, and his eyes fix on Rosemary. Her corn-silk hair, the graceful curve of her neck. He clears his throat. She meets his gaze.

"Well…" she says, her voice trailing away. "I guess I'm gonna go on up and—"

"Rosemary?" interrupts Walter.

"Yes?"

"Ever since the first second I saw you, you've been on my mind. It was like, you were there and I just, I wanted, I… Rosemary, I was wondering: Would you, ah, would you like to take a little walk? Just a walk. Just to talk. That's all. I need that. Just to talk to you a while."

Rosemary meets his eyes, watery, blue, hopeful. *Not a bad guy,* she thinks. *A little neurotic, a little confused. He seems to have a little crush on me. That's sweet.* She feels a rush of emotion. Not sexual, not exactly motherly, but something tender. She reaches up, palms his cheek. "How far you think it is to that pier?"

"I've basically been really several notches above where I usually am," says Walter, home now a few weeks later. "I'm pretty happy. I feel good. And I've noticed, when I'm out and about, when I look at people, I have—I almost want to believe that all these people are also swingers. Like at the grocery store, the post office. I know that they're not, but I really want to believe that they are. I don't know why. I find myself smiling at people. I hope it lasts.

"I tried to get something going with Rosemary, but nothing was gonna happen. It didn't happen. But that's okay. I still had a great time. I'm happy that I took the time and energy to talk to her for a while. Just getting the chance to talk to her was enough. It worked out that you don't have to do everything your mind thinks you want to. I was so relieved and so happy just to have that half hour to walk up the beach and talk. It was kind of a real personal little encounter. A real little gift.

"In a way I think that I decided we'll just save it. Me and Rosemary. Someday at another gathering, we'll meet again, we'll get together. We'll have our chance. We'll—"

Walter gets quiet a moment. Something has occurred to him. Finally, he breaks the silence. "By the way—do you know what state she lives in?"

THE PORN
IDENTITY

When his wife decamps from the household, leaving his life and his bank account in tatters, our hero takes a much-needed assignment traveling the country in search of… retired porn starlets. From Nina Hartley's toy-filled dungeon, to Kay Taylor Parker's spirit-filled studio, to Asia Carrera's split-level hideaway in the mountains north of Las Vegas: How one man gets his mojo back.

I am somewhere around Barstow on the edge of the desert when the Motrin finally kicks in—the electric pain scorching down the back of my leg begins to subside; once again I can feel my foot on the gas pedal. The ache in my heart is another matter. I remind myself to breathe.

Three hours down, four to go, the best car my money can lease. The sky is big, blue and cloudless. The atmosphere is fragrant. My tunes are cranked, an inspiring anthem by the artist Milez called "We Have Hope." I've played it six or seven times already, or maybe 10, I don't know. It might have something to do with the message of the song. Or it might have to do with the fact that Milez is my son—it's something he recorded at the conclusion of a long holiday weekend in the house that used to belong to him and his family but now just belongs to him and his dad. I have 450 miles of highway to cover, spanning four states, hopefully before nightfall. The last stretch, through Arizona and into southern Utah, is said to be treacherous; I've been advised to get through the soaring, weathered canyons before the temperature drops and the road freezes. As I will learn, fatalities happen— lives torn asunder. There are all kinds of ways.

That I've left this particular part of my mission for last now seems prophetic. But then again, everything about this assignment has been weirdly synchronistic. There I was, suffering through the latter stages of a swift and painful divorce, a middle-aged man facing single life after 20 years with the same woman—a recovering cuckold, damaged goods, the male animal at his lowest.

A tornado of anger and resentment and powerlessness swirled through my inner space, turning everything gritty and gray, and all these motherfuckers with their hands in my pants, massaging my misery, waiting for their gusher to come in. Just yesterday I was signing over my assets, three decades worth of pension and gifts and savings. That the Notary Public was a kind lady who worked in the local branch of Mail Boxes Etc. seemed somehow fitting, more irony to stoke the clichéd satire that had become my reality.

For months I've felt as if I've been operating on safe mode—you can give me commands and make me function, but everything seems dull and slow and monochromatic. I wander through my house, going from room to room. I don't know what the hell I'm doing. Putting the scissors away. Emptying the trash. Folding laundry. Shopping for groceries. Making lunch. Changing passwords. Worrying about the future—college for my son, retirement for me. Retirement! I always imagined I'd grow old with her—in some ways, to be honest, it was a scenario that didn't thrill me. At least now I get to sleep in the bed by myself. She used to take up three quarters of the damn thing, which was kind of metaphorical for my life with her—me sleeping on the itty-bitty edge of the big antique bed that had been in my family for 90 years.

And then, serendipitously, an e-mail arrives from the venerable Rabbit. They want me to hit the road. They want to give me money. They want me to track down... Retired porn stars.

You're fucking kidding me, right?

At high noon the Mojave Desert shimmers in all directions. My speedometer is holding steady at 80; cars are passing on my left like I'm standing still. Twisted Joshua trees stand here and there like prickly, gawking townsfolk, stooped and wringing their hands, bearing silent witness to my tortured thoughts. There is snow on the mountaintops; sculpted ridges and balancing rocks landscape the middle distance; a palette of rich reds, strong browns, wan tans —a tribute to nature's powerful and uncluttered sense of color and design. The intro to "We Have Hope" starts up again. I sing along with the chorus. Maybe I *do* have hope, after all.

As you might imagine, finding retired porn starlets turned out to be... not so easy. I left emails on websites, texted blind cell numbers, sent out Facebook messages. Nothing. And then one afternoon, sitting stuporous in my chair, fretting, wondering what the hell I'd gotten myself into, I got an idea.

I went up to the garage and dug into some boxes, found some old paper files, pulled up a few names of ancient contacts. Perhaps in no other arena would my decades-old status as a biographer of the seminal porn star John Holmes serve as a helpful distinction. Every world has its own constellation of reality, its own pantheon of gods. Most of the people I was trying to find didn't particularly want to be found. I was willing to leverage whatever I had.

Luckily, it turned out that my old contacts were still my contacts—not always a sure thing in my business. As it happens, it *does* matter how you comport yourself. It matters how you treat people. It matters how you leave things, how you choose to word your sentences. People remember—even after twenty years.

And so it was that I found myself one evening at the historic Sportsman's Lodge in Studio City, CA, at a memorial wake for John Leslie, one of the great founding fathers of the porn industry, which is what the pornographers like to call the business of X-rated movies. Everyone you could imagine was there, from Ron Jeremy to Holly Hollywood, a room full of Triple-X history, past and present. As the evening wore on, as testimonials were given (even Rocco Siffredi via Skype from Italy), as the liquor flowed from the cash bar and prescription vials of medical marijuana were produced, introductions were made and conversation flowed. Numbers were exchanged. In short order I found myself transported once again into the netherworld of professional sex workers and its vast network of loveable odd fellows.

Over the next three months I drove nearly 2,000 miles. I met Kay Taylor Parker at her little cottage by the sea. For a small fee (I insisted) she performed upon me something called a Body Touch session; the previous day, we dined in a tony restaurant—Maria Shriver, the wife of the former Governor of California, was seated only a muffin-throw away.

Nina Hartley and her second hubby, Ira, a writer and a director of bondage films, occupy a loft space/dungeon happily overlooking a lake. If you go to a dinner party at their house, Nina might be wearing this apparatus called a pony head harness. You will probably have your group sex first, and then eat after, since nobody likes to fuck on a full stomach, she'd explain.

Amber Lynn turned up at the luxe, ground floor restaurant at the Viceroy Hotel in a blue designer frock that complimented beautifully her fetching blue eyes. For three hours, over a delicious seared-tuna salad, she held forth on her life and the lessons learned, the tricky job of navigating between her porn self and the real woman inside, the girl who had her fun and her issues, the woman who wants legitimacy and a normal life. Sure she made fuck films and danced naked at the best strip clubs across the country. Sure she had a nasty penchant for alcohol and smoking cocaine. But now she's been sober for eleven years. Why can't she get a date?

The asphalt highway ribbons out before me. I pass through an Indian reservation, clusters of shacks and old busses and motor homes baking on the hillsides. I push my thoughts ahead, to the woman at the end of the Interstate. I never even thought I'd be making this part of the trip.

From the beginning it was clear that the golden ticket in this X-rated lottery was Asia Carrera, one of porno's first Asian goddesses. Half German, half Japanese, she was a child prodigy who played piano at Carnegie Hall twice before the age of 15—and then ran screaming to the dark side to escape the expectations of her overbearing parents. (Tiger moms, take note: This is what can happen when you push too hard.)

In her films Carrera is forever captured as she was in her prime: five feet eight inches tall, with geisha girl eyes, six-pack abs, a cheerleader's well-muscled ass—which, incidentally, she never gave away on film until she co-produced, co-directed, wrote the script and owned the rights. She appears to orgasm easily and often; in the throes of passion she is often moved to laugh. There is an aw-shucks quality to her afterglow. I'm not sure I've ever witnessed a porn princess—or anyone—who appears to enjoy fucking more than Carrera.

No wonder she'd been number one on my editor's wish list of potential interviewees.

There was only one problem.

Nobody in the industry had seen or spoken to her in years. She was said to be living in seclusion in southern Utah.

Eventually, working my rejuvenated contacts, I found an e-mail address. We struck up a halting correspondence. She was friendly, but I couldn't get her to commit. This went on for several weeks.

Finally, one week out from the date I'd first mentioned for our interview, still unconfirmed, I forced the issue: "Looking forward to seeing you next week!" I typed.

"I love how you're reminding me all nonchalantly, like I haven't been terrified about the date since the moment you told me," she wrote back.

"I'll be gentle, I promise."

"You sure we can't do this by e-mail?"

"In person is better—more accurate."

"C'mon," she chided. "Nobody ever won a Pulitzer for talking to porn stars."

"I'm just a guy whose wife cheated and left. I'm sure I'm more scared of you than you are of me. I'll be gentle if you will."

And then—nothing.

No reply.

Shit!

Had I played my cards wrong? A good journalist knows: It's not about you, it's about your subject. Maybe in my state of emotional disarray I was slipping a little bit. Maybe I'd revealed too much of myself, too soon.

The next day, an email appeared in my box. With a sense of dread, I clicked and opened.

"Wow. I had a dream that we hooked up, NOT kidding. Then I woke up and asked myself, 'Where the heck did THAT come from? The guy's married!' And now you tell me your wife has left you? Oh no! LOL!"

LOL, indeed.

In the off-kilter afterglow of my Body Touch session, I lingered on a comfortable divan chatting with Kay Taylor Parker. A busty redhead wearing an aquamarine sweater to match her sparkling eyes, she is best remembered for her highly charged incest scenes in the 1980 porno classic *Taboo*.

Parker was known in her day as the Prude of Porn. With her British accent and air of innocence, she seemed a little too proper to be in fuck films, despite her 38DDs. She was 33 years old when she entered the biz, a well-traveled British Navy brat who'd arrived in San Francisco during the Summer of Love. Workshop trained as a thespian, she embarked on a porn career in the interest of acting.

Parker came to prominence at a time when X-rated movies were as much political statement as erotic entertainment—actors took care to leave their clothes in a convenient pile lest the cops raid the set. (The first priority before dashing was always to make sure to gather up the *film*, which was subject to confiscation.) During this era of near-mainstream offerings like *Behind the Green Door* and *Deep Throat*—a time of bushy pubes and long, stilted dialogues between sex scenes—Parker's films (with male co-stars like John Leslie, Mike Ranger, and Tom Byron) were shown mostly in old theaters in city centers around the nation, ornate places frequented by adventurous couples and the proverbial men in overcoats, everyone well spaced among the seats.

In all, Parker starred in fewer than 100 movies in this lifetime, which has thus far spanned 67 years. She is aware, she says, of having lived at least 182 other incarnations since her first arrival on Earth, as a female scientist in ancient Atlantis, a Star Being sent to this planet to "help usher in the God-ing through Fourth Dimensional Ascension." For this latter distinction she has been called the Shirley MacLaine of porn. Today she earns her living as a spiritual practitioner; she may be contacted through her euphonious website.

We sat together in her parlor, decorated with geodes and crystals and potted plants, attended by a number of vocal cats. Through the open, sun-filled window came the scent of flowers and sea air, an Edenic soundtrack of chirping birds. It was the second day of my visit; our lunch and interview yesterday had gone swimmingly, we seemed to be well matched. There was a nurturing vibe about her; I think she felt okay about me, too. Yesterday, within a few minutes of our first hellos, Parker experienced a ringing sensation in her right ear. She paused a moment and raised her eyes to the heavens to confer with a force above—I believe it was the spirit of her mentor, Aaron. "You're being given the thumbs up," she said.

For my Body Touch session, Parker asked me to recline on my back on a massage table, covered by a sheet, one arm exposed. She spoke out loud, though not to me, asking questions of—and getting answers from—a higher source... possibly Aaron? As she muttered, she pushed and poked at the meat of my exposed forearm as if working a keyboard or a set of switches—I got the sense she was toggling through a sort of table of contents in my life.

From there she asked a series of leading questions that prompted answers and more questions. There was something about my leaving my girlfriend to go to college at 18, she said. There was something about my choosing, as a young journalist, to work nights instead of days to advance my career—further confounding the same tortured relationship. There was something about my bedroom—specifically about the bed. It had belonged to my grandparents on my mother's side. They'd slept in it together for more than 60 years of marriage. Having inherited the piece, I'd had it lovingly enlarged by a craftsman when my wife had become pregnant.

And then one morning, without notable provocation, my wife had opened her eyes and proceeded to launch into a tirade about the bed. She hated it. She always hated it. Etc. Etc. Not yet aware of the true cause of her sudden misplaced mania—the *denouement* was still some weeks away—I'd followed her wishes *posthaste*. With the help of my son and an electric drill, the bed was dismantled and garaged.

Working the keyboard of my forearm, mumbling to her higher source, Parker focused on the bed and its role in my personal history. At last she found what she was looking for.

I had a missing piece.

There'd been a rape six generations ago on my mother's side, apparently, back in the old country, Eastern Europe. A splinter of my soul had detached and crossed over. Meaning that I was born *incomplete*.

I'd never even suspected.

Maybe that's why I always need to love the wrong girl?

She tapped my forehead with her fingertips, a maneuver of healing, she explained. Tap, tap, tap... It felt like being in the rain.

Now we were sitting together on the couch. I was drinking water as prescribed. Parker was paging through a volume called *Love Cards*, by Robert Lee Camp.

She asked my birth date, looked me up.

"You're a nine of clubs," she announced brightly. She handed me the book. "Read out loud," she ordered.

"Humanitarianism, higher law, universal love, selfishness..." I looked at her questioningly. "What does *dissipation* mean in this context?"

Perplexed, she consulted an alternate guide, a stapled set

of papers. "Always dramatic and dynamic in approach. Leaders in their own field. Very successful as writers. Maybe subject to hampering home conditions but never fail in duty and devotion."

"Hampering home conditions," I repeated. I could feel my face forming itself into a rueful expression. "What about my love life?"

She consulted the pages, regarded me mournfully. "Perhaps you have some other things to do first."

At this point my dry spell had reached a personal record. Was it my destiny to be alone? "How big a part has sex played in *your* life?" I asked.

She smiled beatifically. "I haven't had sex in six years. Even longer before that."

I looked surprised, I suppose. She is still attractive for a woman in her seventh decade. There are still legions of fans on the Internet.

"I've come to the realization that sex isn't all it's made out to be," she said. Like everything, it's the spirit that's important. Whether we're self-pleasuring or interfacing with somebody else, at a core level it's really about a union with God. Or the divine. Or the creator. Or Fred—whatever we want to call that energy.

"Sex has become so hollow today—especially since porno is so huge on the Internet," she continued. "It leads me to believe that more people are sitting at home masturbating than engaging in intimate relationships."

Guilty as charged, I told myself.

She looked at me gravely. "If we could all have sex in the spirit of communion with God, we'd immediately eradicate war on the planet. To me that's what the fourth dimension is all about. It's about union, about communion, about—"

She was interrupted by the sound of wind chimes. Then the cats started up, meowing like crazy.

The door to the outside patio swung open.

"Come in, come in, come in…" Parker sang.

But there was nobody there.

I followed Nina Hartley down a dark hallway on an upper floor of a spooky-cool converted loft building. Her celebrated bubble butt, high and round and sheathed in black leggings, was doing its work ahead of me. Back in the 1980s, Hartley's was known as the Best Ass in Porn. From where I was walking, it showed no signs of decline.

It was our second day together. We'd started with a long drive along surface streets—she prefers to avoid the freeway in her black on black T-Bird convertible—and spent the afternoon at a chic beauty salon on ritzy Montana Avenue—her colorist splits time between Los Angeles and Tel Aviv. After that, she'd appeared on an Internet chat show, "Porn Star Pundits," where heavyweights from the X industry hold forth on news topics of the day. "We are more than just the sum of our genitals, people!" Hartley was compelled to quip. She was joined on the panel by the younger male star Jack Lawrence; besides sharing a reputation for expertise in cunnilingus, it turned out, they are both fallen-away Jews. Off air, they decided their particular talent set had something to do with their culture's strong link between love and eating.

Hartley is one of the more outspoken porn stars, past and present. Her longevity and her status as one of the Erotic Eleven— she was arrested on obscenity charges in 1993 after a benefit performance for the Free Speech Coalition—have conveyed upon her a sort of queenly status. She has the upbeat, ironic, rat-a-tat delivery of a café society intellectual, distinguished by a slight lateral lisp. Throughout our time together, Hartley rarely took a breath, filling the air with genial patter, bright commentary and unconventional opinions—a lot of which make good sense. She described herself, variously, as "a sex-positive feminist," "a heterosexual butch dyke," "a gay man with female parts," "a bisexual exhibitionistic polyamorous person who is by nature emotionally monogramous."

Truly, her verbal skills rival her oral ones.

In some ways, you could say Hartley is an embodiment of the industry's own story arc. Curious about sex from an early age, the bookish girl took herself to see her first X-rated movie at 17 at an art house in San Francisco. The film was an adaptation of one of her favorite erotic novels, first published anonymously in 1887, *The Autobiography of a Flea*. The film version starred early porn gods Jean Jennings, Paul Thomas and John Holmes. In time, Hartley would meet or work with all of them.

Hartley is the daughter of a blacklisted local radio personality and his attractive brunette wife, whom Hartley credits for her ass. Hartley's ice-blue eyes are the heritage of her German Swiss dad, who went into free fall after being outed as a communist. The story is complicated; he ended up at one point finding employment as a short-order cook before her mom became the breadwinner. Her parents were together for 64 years; they worked hard on their marriage. Over time, Hartley explained, the couple investigated all manner of therapeutic options, including primal scream therapy, group therapy, biofeedback, bioenergetics and naked tai chi. At last they found their peace within the teachings of Zen Buddhism. They lived with others in a religious cooperative until recently, when her father died peacefully in a hospice with his family at his bedside. Hartley has eight nieces and nephews, upon whom she dotes. Uterine fibroid tumors and a lack of interest have precluded her own career as a parent.

Born in 1959, Marie Hartman (in everyday life, to maintain her anonymity, she uses at least two *more* different names), was the fourth and last of her parents progeny, a "semi-feral child" raised with "benign neglect." Looking back, the business seems an almost obvious choice for a lonely young girl who grew up in the dark time after her father's fall from grace.

At 24 she entered her first amateur strip contest; she wore satin slippers and used a cream-colored vibrator as a prop— penetration was legal onstage in San Francisco in those wild, pre-AIDS days. She won $200 and a job… in a live peep show. During each shift she had sex with a different woman on a rotating bed in a round room. Along the circumference of the room were booths. Each had a window, a chair, a wastebasket and paper towels. If the guy wished to be visible to the entertainers, he could turn on a light in his booth.

Hartley started doing porn movies in the early 1980s, just as theatrical distribution was giving way to an amazing new home movie device called a VCR. Previously, only the wealthy could watch movies at home. (The poor went to peep shows. You fed a machine with quarters and watched black-and-white film on a tiny screen—just as the action got heavy, it would shut down and you'd need to insert another quarter.) The first porno I ever saw was played on an expensively-rented movie projector in the rec room of my college fraternity house. The year was 1975. I remember the film being fuzzy and breaking several times; the actor wore black socks; the girl was doughy and hairy and nondescript.

The first straight-to-video films still boasted decent pay, large budgets and discernible story lines. As video drove the X industry more mainstream—with revenue in the billions over two golden decades—Hartley crossed over as well. A nurse by education (dancing and adult-film work paid her nursing school tuition), she frequently lectures on sex and politics, has appeared on *The Oprah Winfrey Show*, has written a sex guide- book and produced a handful of instructional videos. In 1997 Hartley won a part in the mainstream movie in *Boogie Nights*. She was critically lauded for her turn as William H. Macy's unfaithful wife. (He finds her getting fucked missionary style on a sun-bleached and dusty driveway, surrounded by a crowd of onlookers. Between thrusts, she chides him for embarrass- ing her by interrupting.)

At 52, Hartley still does several scenes a month to make ends meet—MILF stuff and girl-on-girl. Enthusiast sites on the web credit Hartley with appearances in more than 850 differ- ent titles.

For nearly 20 years, as she became more well-known, making movies and touring the country as a featured stripper, Hartley lived in a three-way union—two women and a man named Dave, a father figure she met at 19 who'd helped her get into film. Dave came with a girlfriend named Bobby. Since Nina was bisexual ("I got into porno because that's where the naked women were," she likes to say), this arrangement seemed perfect.

And for a time it was—or at least it seemed like it was, the blue smoke and mirrors of love's twisted heart.

"Some people blow their money on a bad drug habit," she said, unlocking the door to her apartment. "I blew mine on a bad marriage."

She led me into the great room. A bank of windows overlooked the city skyline. Nearby was an expansive green park, at the center of which was a lake with a fountain. To one side of the loft space was an eclectic kitchen—the funky, lived in, makeshift variety typical to loft conversions. The walls opposite the windows were lined with books; the top shelf was chokablock with martial-style caps—the type worn by police chiefs and military dictators with lots of do-dads and crosses and shiny gold trim. Nina's pony head harness was resting on an antique wig form, awaiting its next call to action.

"When I first got divorced, I said I would probably end up alone with cats and fuck buddies," Hartley said. "I never thought I'd be married again. Ever."

"I kind of feel like that now," I told her. "Except for the cats and the fuck buddies."

Hartley regarded me piteously through her chunky square-framed glasses—magnified, her eyes are like twin sapphires. "It's tough in our society," she said soothingly. "We're supposed to marry for love. Your partner is supposed to be your best friend and your soul mate and the best lover you ever had. And that's supposed to last your entire life."

She gestured as any proud homeowner would, bidding me to follow her on a tour of the long rectangular space she occupies with her husband, Ira, also known as Ernest Greene, a porn pundit and director of bondage films. "I guess I was lucky," she continued. "I met my husband during a threesome, so we had non-monogamy as the starting point. We love threesomes together. In that way we are *so* compatible."

Down the hallway, there are partitioning walls but no

doors, except on the two bathrooms, so every room has a view out the large windows. She showed me a bedroom, another bedroom, and then… the office/playroom.

On one side is a desk, a phone, files.

The rest of the room features, in no particular order: A stainless-steel stand-up cage (three feet square by six feet high), an X frame for flogging, a spanking horse, a bondage bed, a custom-rigged suspension pulley, countersunk floor rings for restraint purposes and a "bounce wall"—a thickly padded section of wall against which to throw people, also known as a vertical trampoline. There is also a wall of tools arranged neatly on a home-workshop-type pegboard: whips, chains, paddles, riding gear (some by very high-end European luxury-goods houses), leather cuffs, padlocks. And of course a cabinet of safer-sex supplies: condoms, gloves, lube, an assortment of Hitachi Magic Wands—Hartley has never come easily… she has a high threshold, she says.

Entering the space, I nearly tripped over a knee-high leather boot, one of a number of pairs scattered around the rubber floor (for easy cleanup). Apologizing in the manner of a housewife entertaining an unexpected guest, Hartley made quick work of lining up and straightening the boots.

"Ira is *much* kinkier than I am. *Much kinkier.* He's 100% kinky," Hartley said, not missing a beat as she policed the floor, picking up a riding crop, some wadded tissues, a tube of lube. "I'm kinky, sure. I like a little power exchange, a little orgy, some girl on girl—I can even go for some bi-boy action. I'm a universal adapter. If it involves naked adults, count me in. I'll watch, I'll help, I'll hold your foot, I'll hold your coat. *Whatever.*

"But with Ira, if it's not BDSM, he ain't interested. *Period.* He'll keep his clothes on, thank you very much. That's why he supports me having a lover, my boyfriend, whatever you wanna call him—I've known him since high school and he's pure vanilla. And I do the same for Ira—he has this partner with whom he completely shares his sexual nature. She is one hundred percent masochistic-submissive. I know it's good for him; I want him to have it. It makes it easier for both of us to return to the other at the end of every day. I have to tell you: the idea that I still want to make love to the same man after ten years blows my mind."

I looked around the playroom, wanting to take it in, but not wanting to seem like a tourist. "You're lucky," I managed. I meant it.

"It took me a long time, but now I understand what it means to create your own reality," she said. "For so many years I didn't understand anything about being in a healthy relationship. Things spiraled out of control. It got to the point where I was lying, withholding and cheating. If I had been raised to be more honest and ethical and not a liar, I would have been able to go home and face my ex sooner and say, 'You know what? I've met somebody. The relationship we have doesn't work for me.' But I didn't know how to have that difficult conversation. I didn't know how to stand up for myself. I didn't know how to operate from a position of strength. Instead, I lied."

Her words resonated. There'd been a lot of lying in my own deceased marriage. I've had trouble trying to figure out how my "best friend" could do me like that.

Sensing my grief, Hartley took a step closer and put her hand on my shoulder. We looked out the window, past the cage and the bondage rack. The sun was setting over a green park; the sky was pink and orange.

"What are you doing for dinner?" she asked.

I looked up from my booth in the restaurant at the Viceroy Hotel and caught sight of Amber Lynn, striding toward me across the high-gloss oak plank flooring like a super model plying a long runway, wearing a pair of gold Michael Kors pumps with four-inch heels and a short, stunning Alice + Olivia dress, the electric blue of which harmonized beautifully with the Caribbean blue of her eyes. Her silken blonde hair, expensively cut, floated back and away from her sculpted face. It seemed as though a spot-light was following her as she moved, setting her aglow; I was reminded of one of those slow-motion dream sequences you see sometimes in movies. Time stops—for the horny teenager... the 40-year-old virgin... the hapless divorcee—as the lust object enters the room.

Lynn was known in her day, along with her friends Ginger Lynn and Traci Lords, as one of the Golden Goddesses of Porn. If you add up the numbers, Lynn probably started in the industry when she was underage, just as Lords did so notoriously before becoming a legitimate actress. Lynn was an original Vivid Video girl, though not a contract player. With her mid-1980s nimbus of blonde curls, this petite Melanie Griffith look-alike reigned over video's glam years of glossy box covers, high salaries and rock-star perks—limos, makeup artists, hotel suites, Peruvian cocaine... all of it at a time when the Reagan and Bush administrations were spending billions on wars against drugs and immorality.

On-screen, Amber Lynn was as tough as nails, a no-nonsense dirty girl known for her snarl; she seemed as likely to bite off a dick as to suck on it. The bulk of her films were made between the mid-1980s and the mid-1990s. She has 373 titles to her credit, according to the web. Early on, she had a reputation for being particular: it was said she wouldn't do anal or bi-racial scenes. Later, during her darker years, there seemed to be fewer rules. After quitting film, Lynn worked for more than a decade as a featured dancer in strip clubs all over the United States and Canada, making as much as $25,000 a week, some of it in the form of $1 bills, hauled out each night in garbage bags.

After a run-in with the law, Lynn hit rock bottom and began the long process of turning her life around. Now 47 (48, according to Wikipedia and other sources), she's been sober for 11 years. She is a real estate agent specializing in luxury properties. She also works as a personal recovery assistant, known as a sober companion, counseling detoxing drug users—some of them young porn starlets.

As she sat over a lunch of seared-tuna salad and bubbly water, Lynn's story unfolded—porn's cautionary tale. One of her mentors, the critic and historian Bill Margold, another member of the Erotic Eleven, has always called the business "The Playpen of the Damned." Looking back over her life, Lynn's path seems almost predestined.

Laura Lynn Allen grew up in Orange County, California, the daughter of a retired Air Force officer and his brittle wife. The couple had two boys and then a girl who died, at the age of two, of a previously undetected heart defect. Lynn was conceived as a "replacement child," she explained, picking at her salad. "My brothers and my family were very overprotective."

The sadness of the little girl's death cast a deep shadow over the household. When Lynn was three, her father was discovered to have a second brood with another woman. There was a divorce. Lynn's mother had a nervous breakdown and was institutionalized. Lynn was sent to foster care. There was physical abuse.

When she was seven, Lynn reunited with her mother. Shortly thereafter, they were driving on the interstate after a holiday vacation when high winds caused a cement mixer to jackknife in front of their car. Lynn was thrown clear of the wreckage. Her mother was nearly decapitated; she died at the scene. The young girl witnessed all. "At that moment, part of me split," she said. "That's what children do. They kind of split emotionally so they don't suffer the trauma."

Lynn's father moved into his old house with his new family—by now he had four boys with the stepmom. In total, there were eight boys and Lynn. When she was 11, her father died from alcoholism and heart failure. Her stepmother carried on, seemingly as best she could.

Entering her teens, Lynn was "a pudgy, bucktoothed" tomboy, by necessity one of the guys. It was a small town. Everybody knew the misfortunate Allen clan; several of the boys were in car clubs, popular at the time. "I started going to the gym with my brother (who would go on to become the porn actor and director Buck Adams; a hard partier, Adams died from heart and liver failure at age 53).

As she approached her teenage years, "I guess I kind of blossomed," Lynn said. "I was maturing, losing my baby fat. I

developed this rocking little body. I started doing fitness modeling and bikini modeling—I would be in a bathing suit down at
the Orange County Raceway, that kind of thing, or I would do
hot body contests. I had a fake ID, and my brother was the door-
man at this club where they held the contests, and it was his job
to check the IDs. So he would let me into the club and I would
enter. I had, like, *no* breasts—anybody who knows my original
stuff knows I had very little up there. But these contests were all
about the lower body. I had these great abs, great legs, the great
ass, the whole package. The purse was like $350 to $500 dollars,
which was a ton of money to us. I would cut everybody in on
the deal, and we would party for the weekend. That's how we
got our money.

"At one point, I remember, the first g-strings game out,"
she continued. "Nobody had ever worn g-strings on the beach
in Newport. They hired me, I think I was 16, to skate up and
down the boardwalk in a g-string. And I remember when I did
it, it was like, WOW. It was such a rush! I mean, people stopped
and stared. Heads were turning. After that, I kind of became
addicted. I remember getting off on the attention. Really, really
getting off. This was my first taste of, like, 'Wow, this is making
me feel… really hot.'"

She took a bite of her tuna and chewed, reflecting. "See,
I grew up being known as little Lynnie. I always felt small and
unsexy in this name, always overprotected by my brothers, the
replacement child trying to live up to the perfect memory of my
dead sister. As I started to feel the power of being noticed by
men, oh my God, I just wanted to shed this whole image of the
broken little girl."

She laughed wickedly, the insight of age. "The funny thing
was, I thought I was so wild, but I was not very sexually daring
at all. I was strutting my stuff but I was a not a slut by any
means. I was an innocent—we did like backseat petting and,
and you know, rode on our boyfriends' motorcycles and did all
these things, but it wasn't like I was having intercourse with
boys. There was a lot of stuff I didn't know anything about. We

weren't even giving blowjobs."

Lynn embraced this new, empowered self and started pushing her boundaries. Venturing an hour north to Hollywood, she became a regular at rock clubs on the Sunset Strip like the Rainbow Room and the Starwood. She partied hard. She lost her virginity. She got an agent. She posed for *Penthouse* magazine and was paid a healthy sum. She met the wife of *Hustler* founder Larry Flynt, the star-crossed Althea, and became her pal, riding around town in the Flynt's white stretch limo, a naked woman airbrushed on the side. Years later, Lynn's affinity for the rock scene would come full circle when she'd dance on tour with Motley Crue and Guns n Roses—before a crowd of 50,000 at Wembly Stadium in the UK. For a time she was romantically involved with Arrowsmith sideman Tom Gimble.

When she was 17, Lynn was sent by her agent to a "go-see" for a movie. She knew it was not a Hollywood film; the director was a well-known porn veteran. In those days there was a difference between being a naked pinup model and being a porn actress. There was legitimate work for girls who did nude/no sex, even in X rated films. That's what Lynn was there to audition for.

Sitting down with the director in the opening moments of their conversation, Lynn recalled, the director said: "You seem nervous. Do you want a hit?"

Even though she was young, Lynn (and Lynnie, too) had plenty of experience partying. "We drank whatever booze we could steal off our parents. We used to buy kegs and put them in the back of my brother's mini truck and go out to the desert. We did LSD. We did mushrooms. We smoked a lot of grass. It was home grown. My brother grew it. We had pipes all over the house. That's how we rolled."

Now the director handed her a glass bong. She took it without hesitation, assuming it was a marijuana pipe.

"I remember as I was taking the hit, I looked down into the bowl —and I'll never forget this: there was a white rock on top that was melting into the weed as it burned. And I thought, "What the hell is that?"

A dark look crossed her face, which shows ample evidence of a plastic surgeon's work. "I'll never forget the way it hit me the first time. It was like, *Oh. My. God.*

"Anybody who has ever freebased knows the feeling, especially if you've been an addict. It's as if the birds are singing. The light is brighter. All of a sudden I'm no longer this gangly nervous teenager. I'm sitting there going, 'Oh wow!'

"They say you can't rape the willing, and I was completely willing... I was completely open. Because I came from a dysfunctional family, I didn't have really good boundaries. I'm the kind of person, If I'm standing on a cliff and I'm looking down, I might be thinking, you know, 'Wow, it looks like it could really be good fun to just jump off the fucking cliff with no parachute.' That's always been sort of innate in me my whole life—I will do things that are complete insanity."

The next day, still high on freebase cocaine, Lynn filmed her first movie.

The day after that, while preparing to film her second, she walked into a house and met porn legend Jamie Gillis, who would become her longtime partner and the love of her life.

A week later, she met Ginger Lynn—who promptly took her hand, led her to a chaise lounge by a pool and made passionate love to her. It was her first experience with another woman. The two would remain close for years.

And thus Amber Lynn was born—the amber for the sun-kissed color of her fresh and supple skin. The drugs and alcohol would continue for nearly two decades. Little Lynnie was successfully eradicated.

"Cut to a few years later," Lynn said, using her fork to separate the waxed beans and pickled red onions from the warm white new potatoes. "Me, Ginger Lynn and Traci Lords were all on a set together. We're partying in our dressing room. And we started, like, competing over who was going to do what in the film—who was going to do more than the others. We were all sort of friends, but at the same time, we were all competitive. We're all like, *How am I going to outdo these other girls?* Cause we all thought, you know, *I'm the girl who's number one.*"

Lynn shook her head abashedly, an old vet telling war stories. "We all outdid ourselves *that* day. We all did stuff we'd never done. I shot a DP, a double penetration, and Ginger shot a DP, and then I think Traci shot... no, I didn't do a DP. Ginger did a DP, and I did..."

She threw up her hands; her Donna Karan bracelets jingle-jangled.

Who can remember?

"I started out drinking Ketel One and slicing off crystals of Peruvian rock," Lynn said. "I wound up broken down, drinking Kamchatka out of a half-pint stashed in the bottom of my purse, with my crack pipe stuffed in the lining of my jacket. By the time it was done I was a can't-get-myself-out-of-my-closet type of drug addict."

And I thought I had problems.

We talked for hours. She spoke about her charity efforts, her work with addicts, her desire to be seen as a legitimate player in entertainment history rather than as a closeted embarrassment. "It's just sex," she said. "Everybody does it, people! And everybody watches it? So what's the problem?"

The sun moved across the sky. The light softened. The longer we spoke, the more beautiful she seemed, the more human, the more real. At last the restaurant was empty. I paid the check and walked her out to the valet to get her car.

"Amber Lynn was all the things Lynnie never was," she said as we waited in the portico. "For a while, that's all I cared about; killing off Lynnie. But now I've come full circle. I don't want to be Lynnie, but I don't want to be Amber anymore, either. I just want to be myself."

She paused for a moment, considering what she was about to say next. "Not so long ago, I was living with somebody. We had this huge blowout, and he became abusive and I had to call the cops. And after I put down the phone, you know, he yelled at me, he was like: 'Nobody's going to believe you. You were in fuck films.' He was really trying to belittle me.

"But when I look back on my time in porn, I'm proud of what I did, especially the charity stuff I did for the Youth AIDS Foundation. You can say what you want about porn, but back then we were rock stars; the rock star and the porn-star image began to kind of look alike. We were no longer a seedy little underground business. We were in everybody's living room. Anybody who was hip, it was like *the* thing to have a porn collection. And if you collected anything, you had to have the top three women in porn—Traci Lords, Ginger Lynn and Amber Lynn."

"There should be a Mount Rushmore of Porn," I joked. "You'd be right up there."

She smiled wickedly. "When the cops came to take that abusive roommate of mine away in handcuffs, I thought to myself, *What are they going to remember you for in twenty years, shit bird?*"

Her car appeared. I tipped the valet and opened the door myself. Lynn's dress was short. Her amber-colored, perfectly toned thighs scissored open and closed.

She caught me staring.

I felt myself blush.

"Give me a call if you have any follow-up questions," she said coquettishly.

And then she was gone down the long driveway.

Standing before the limited offerings in my motel room closet, I consider the options for my big night out with Asia Carrera. If you can believe it, my date tonight, this beautiful hapa cyborg and multiorgasmic member of Mesa, a veteran of more than 350 X-rated titles, hasn't been out to dinner with a man in five years. I'm determined to pull out all the stops.

It is late in the afternoon of my second full day in southern Utah. I feel like I've driven through a time warp, a small town from the past—big families, low crime, everyone smiling, everything closed on Sundays, the sharp white spires of the Mormon temple gleaming against the awesome red rocks. The fact that porn is illegal here and that I'm visiting a porn star has not been left unconsidered. Neither has the fact that certain of my medical prescriptions aren't valid across state lines. I have dressed thus far to suit my surroundings—sometimes it's best to blend in.

From the moment she picked me up yesterday in her aging SUV, her hair frizzy and pulled back, her mismatched workout suit stained with food, her figure quite a bit fuller than in the movies, we'd sort of clicked. If it were true that deep intellectual communion could be included on the list of the fun activities that dwell under the rubric of sexual congress—if intense, revelatory sharing of intimate personal details by two consenting adults were considered a type of sex—you could say that Asia Carrera and I had been going at it like a pair of college kids: nonstop, all over town, all over her house, sitting, standing, eating, walking, driving.

We talked and brunched at Cracker Barrel and Denny's. We sat together for hours in her great room and talked and shared tears. She talked as she autographed naked pictures for me and my son. (What I really wanted was a ceramic Asia figurine, but I was too embarrassed to ask.) We talked and ate dinner with her two children at IHOP—that was me completing the Rockwell-esqe family picture, holding the hand of her blond-mulleted four-year-old son as we crossed the parking lot together. The older child, six-year-old Catty (short for Catalina, the island where her parents became engaged), is a miniature Asia. She held her own in the conversation, chattering away on diverse topics, including the subject of her second-grade class, which she attends with kids who are two and three years older. (The school's principal wanted to skip her yet another grade, but Carrera worried about the social effects. It's bad enough it's a Christian school and Catty is an avowed atheist.)

A brilliant and somewhat manic personality, with an IQ over 150, Carrera owns six cats. They come and go, meowing and spatting among themselves like the female cast of a low-budget porno, through a little cat door in the great room of her overlarge investment property in a semi-rural housing development, where some of the neighbors keep horses. The cats bring in dead birds, bunnies, lizards, chipmunks, scorpions, the occasional snake. Sometimes the birds come back to life. There is a high ceiling. Carrera has to drag a ladder from the garage and climb up there to catch them.

There is seemingly nothing she can't teach herself to do. She is the woman you'd like to be paired with when the end-times come—a glance through her bookshelves reveals a survivalist's bent for self-sufficiency. She riffs on the geology of the surrounding area. The use of a weed whacker. The market for renovating and flipping houses. The several fortunes won and lost investing in Latin American stocks, the high-tech bubble and online gambling. The curious phenomenon of something called a pink sock, an unintended result of anal sex. And the fascinating clinical details of her easy-to-reach G-spot.

Born a Jessica and raised on the Jersey Shore, Carrera was the eldest of four kids. Her mom is German; her dad is Japanese—"a perfect storm of iron will and overachievement," Carrera said. There were dance lessons, piano lessons, spelling championships, math Olympiads, the two appearances at Carnegie Hall before 15. Carrera wanted to be a pianist but her parents wanted her to go to Harvard; they made her quit piano to concentrate on her studies.

"My father is the brilliant one," Asia said. "He's practically autistic. He's definitely Asperger's. And he would come home and go into his computer room and close the door. He never said more than two sentences to me or expressed any emotion or had any input as a parent. My mother was not as smart as me—she didn't know what to do with me. By the time I was in fourth or fifth grade, my mother couldn't do the math anymore. She thought she could make me perform better by punishing me more or beating me harder. That was all she knew how to do.

"To her, an A-minus wasn't good enough. If I came in second place in the school spelling bee, my mom would be like, 'Why didn't you come in first? Who came in first? Why aren't you like them?' I won more awards than anybody in my school. I still have them all in a freaking book in the garage. And I never got a word of praise from her. Nothing was never ever *ever* good enough. I was always feeling like a turd. I tried to kill myself so often that it was just a joke. My friends were like, 'Ha ha she tried to kill herself again.' I was in hell. I took up cutting as a hobby because I was always trying to vent pain and anger and frustration. I had slashes all up and down my arm. I was always having my stomach pumped in the hospital. It was just miserable."

At 17, she ran away from home. "I was sleeping with people for a place to stay. I was seriously hungry. I'd ask my friends to bring me some Doritos. But I wouldn't go home. I was stubborn."

She was saved from the streets by a full scholarship to Rutgers University, which included room and board. For spending money she worked as a shot girl in a bar. One night the boss asked her to do a private party. She poured drinks, danced on the bar and came home with $350. Of course it didn't take her long to do the math. She dropped out of college, got a nose job (they called her Big Nose all through high school) and started dancing and modeling. Eventually she flew out to Los Angeles and found her way into porn.

"The things I was doing on the streets made porn seem like paradise. At least in porn I could take my pick of the hot guys and get paid a lot of money to do it and call all the shots and stuff. Porn was a step up for me after leaving home, believe me."

The business proved a perfect fit for Carrera's rare type of genius. "I like being a workaholic. I like being a perfectionist. I like being an overachiever—as long as I'm doing what I want to do. I was able to write all my own scripts, star in my movies, design my box covers and do my own makeup and hair—I even cut my own hair. I did freaking everything. And I would show up with my script memorized. I knew everybody else's lines, too, so I could cue everybody if they forgot their lines without screwing up a take.

"I would even bring wardrobe enough for everybody. It's like, if they said, 'We need a watch this scene, I had three watches in my makeup case. If I ripped my outfit, I was like,

'Hold on! I've got a sewing kit!' I was not the prettiest girl in porn by a long shot but I was easily the most perfectionist. The directors loved me. I would always get a call after every shoot with the director kissing my ass and saying thank you for working so hard, because I did. That's why I got hired so much. They knew when they called me I would show up on time and I would be prepared and I would have everything done and then some."

After working for a year as a Vivid girl, Carrera started making her own films with her first husband, the porn director Bud Lee, who was some twenty years her senior. But even as she enjoyed her success, the demands of fame were crippling. One of the few big porn stars who did not elect to go out on the strip circuit, Carrera harbored a terrible secret: "I was terrified of people."

The more popular she became, the more her public recognition grew... the more difficulty Carrera had being in public places. Making pornos was fine. It was the world that scared her. Just the thought of signing autographs at the annual Consumer Electronics show in Las Vegas would leave her "absolutely terrified. I'd curl up in the shower and just cry. See, I'm a perfectionist. And how can you be perfect in front of all of those people with their cameras for hours on end? Nobody can be perfect for that long. The pressure is unbelievable. I've got lipstick on my teeth, there's a booger coming out of my nose. What if I have to sneeze? Is there toilet paper on my shoe? Is somebody looking up my dress? Is there, is, is there like deodorant coming out of my armpit.

"This is how I am. I have a high IQ. My brain goes very fast. I'm able to extrapolate one million things that can go wrong in the space of just walking out there. It's like bzzzz, my brain short circuits with thoughts of all the things that can go wrong. And I'm trying to prepare for every possible thing that could go wrong. I bring like 10,000 outfits and backup outfits and shoes and backup shoes. It's three days and I've got like 15 outfits and 10 pairs of shoes lined up. And oh my god. And like backup jewelry and backup makeup and, and I take like two hours to get ready."

Carrera vowed to leave porn by the age of 30 with a wad of cash. She followed her plan—for the most part. Bad luck with investments and an addiction to online gambling took her fortune. But at the age of 29 she met Don Lemmon, a fitness guru and nutritionist. Lemmon had approached her about being a spokesmodel for his male-enhancement product. With his long flowing hair and muscles, he was just her type.

Lemmon moved in with Carrera after three days. The pair was engaged after three weeks, married after three months. A few months later Carrera became pregnant with Catty. "It was such a storybook romance. It was just head-over-heels love. It was so amazing."

After Catty was born, the couple moved to southern Utah, a quiet place with good schools and low housing prices. Lemmon and Carrera figured nobody would recognize her in a place where porn was essentially outlawed. And it turned out to be true, mostly—the few people who did recognize her were thrilled to find a kindred spirit in their midst. They bought a house and settled into an idyllic co-dependent, semirural existence. The family was rarely apart. Carrera became pregnant with their second child. Everything was perfect.

And then, in the early morning hours of June 10, 2006, driving home from a business dinner in Las Vegas, Lemmon lost control of his Jeep. His blood alcohol level was found to be almost triple the legal limit.

"The last entry I'd made on my blog was all about how freaking great my life was and how it was like a Cinderella story. I wrote, literally, 'My life is a fairy tale.' And then my next update was, 'Well, the fairy tale is over.'"

Carrera was 32 years old. And eight months pregnant.

"Every day I would wake up as though I'd been kicked in the gut, thinking, *Oh my God, the nightmare is still real; he's still not here.* I would take his urn down and just lie on it and cry and go, 'Daddy, please come home, please come home, please come home.' Catty would come over and she would cry and she would push me off the urn. I didn't want to upset her; she was only 15 months old. And I knew it wasn't good for me to be lying on the floor screaming in hysterics with a baby in my belly. I wasn't in a good place. I was completely co-dependent on Don. I hadn't driven a car in two years. I didn't even go to the store without him. I was scared of the whole world. I'm socially phobic. It was so hard on me."

Then she found out that Lemmon was broke.

"Don had told me he was doing really well and business was great. I wasn't working except for my website; he was paying all the bills, I was just using my money for play. Everything was cool. Or so I thought. It turned out that he was like robbing Peter to pay Paul, and he was juggling all these debts because he wanted to keep me in the lifestyle that I was accustomed to. It turned out we had $2,000 in the bank, which was like enough to pay one mortgage payment, and that was it. And then all these debts, including like $30,000 owed to the IRS and then all his product makers are calling me up and saying, 'Well, he owes me for this and he owes me for that.' I was like, 'I don't have any money to give you people, and I'm grieving my husband and I'm freaking pregnant and my world just freaking fell apart.' Oh god, it was such a nightmare."

Carrera went through the paperwork necessary to give up her unborn son for adoption. "I didn't think I could handle it. I was just such a mess. I was like, 'I've got a 15 month old, no husband, no money. I'm probably going to lose my house. How am I going to take care of another kid? So I found somebody who was going to adopt him. She was half Asian and had a white husband and had a son who looked just like Catty. I was like 'Okay, this is going to be perfect.'"

As it happened, Carrera went into labor two weeks early. For months, even before Lemmon's death, she'd been planning to deliver her child at home. She decided to proceed.

"I set Catty up with her sippy cup, watching a *Wiggles* video in the next room. And then I got the shower curtain down on the floor and all the tools and stuff laid out. I tried to do a water birth in the backyard, but the water was fucking freezing. I'm sitting there thinking, *This is not relaxing.* Then Catty climbs into the pool with all her clothes on, so then I have to take Catty and change her into warm dry clothes—meanwhile I'm having contractions. I called the midwife, and I was like, 'You know what? I guess it's time to go to the hospital.' But then I got on my knees over the birthing pad, and this little head pops out of me. I'm like, *Oh my God! There's a baby down there.* So I just delivered him.

"And there he was. He was lying on the shower curtain and the towel, and I'm taking pictures of him—he's still connected to me by the umbilical cord and I'm taking pictures. And I've got these great pictures of Catty looking at him, like, *What is that thing?* It was so cute. She was so small, looking at the baby, and there's little Devin, and he's like covered in ketchup and mustard.

Then I carried Devin into the bathroom and took pictures of us together in the mirror, and he's still connected to me by the cord and I'm taking pictures in the mirror of us. And by the time I got him cleaned up and swaddled, the doorbell rang. It's the midwife: 'I'm here!' And I said, 'Well you can go now, I'm all done.' And I open the door and I have the baby in my arms. And she's like, 'Oh my god!'

"The funny thing is: Had Devin come on time, he would have been adopted. It was just a freak of fate that he came two weeks early. But everything happens for a reason, right? It's weird, but the whole ordeal of the birth was exactly what I needed to make me feel strong enough to be able to handle raising two kids by myself. I thought, If I can birth a baby by myself, I can do this without Don. I was like, I am Superwoman; I can do this. It was an incredible high."

Then another twist:

About a year after Devin's birth, a statement came for a life insurance policy premium. She'd been bugging Lemmon to get one. Turns out he actually had. Due to the circumstances of his death, the policy paid double.

"Right now, my life is my kids, period," she said, standing

by the fish tank at her house, feeding a giant one-eyed pacu named Pacu. "I don't have the time and energy to dedicate to a relationship. My kids don't have another parent. They don't have other family here. They don't have anybody but me, and I'm a perfectionist workaholic. If that means putting my own needs aside, that's absolutely fine. I'm totally cool with that. It's as though Catty is the Asia that could have been if she hadn't been abused by her parents. And Devin is such a special little dude. I'll be Mommy until they're 18. That's fine with me."

The elevator dings open and I cross the lobby of my motel, which doubles in the morning as the site of an all-you-can-eat breakfast buffet. I decide to damn the local sensibilities and go with Full Writer Drag: black dress shirt, black jeans, black leather car coat, high top Dr. Martens. Asia hasn't been on a dinner date with a man in over five years. She deserves the full treatment, does she not?

I wave to the clerk behind the front desk; he's been so nice, this towering, apple cheeked Mormon lad with a friendly smile.

Only right now he's not smiling.

He looks as though he's just seen the devil.

Before I can react, someone links my arm. Asia Carrera towers over me in four-inch fuck-me pumps. She is wearing a long blue floral dress with a plunging neckline; her cinematic 36Cs are on full display. Her hair has been carefully coiffed; her eyes are vividly awash in her trademark blue eye shadow and thick China-doll mascara—just like in all her old photos.

Dumbstruck, I'm led through the automatic doors. I recover my wits enough to remember to walk her around to the driver's side.

"Just because I'm all dressed up doesn't mean anybody's getting lucky," she purrs.

"I feel like I'm already lucky," I tell her, buckling my seat belt. It sounds like a good line. But I think I really mean it.

Sure, I have some big-time hurt to get over. I have to find a way to finance the future for myself and my son—and to pay

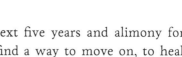

"equalizing payments" for the next five years and alimony for the next seven. And I have to find a way to move on, to heal the wounds—presumably I'll be able to trust someone again; presumably I'll want to share my life with another human being. I still find myself crying at times; I still find myself spiriting around the house like a ghost, moving from place to place, trying to figure out where the fuck I'm trying to go.

But you know what? I think I'll be okay. Fuck my ex for fucking me over like that—she'll be sorry someday, I'm sure of it. I'll make more money. I'll love my son; already our bond is much stronger than it ever was. I'll turn the hurt I've suffered into wisdom; it will make me a better writer and a better human being. If Asia, Nina, Amber and Kay can transcend their various trials and miseries, certainly I can too.

"Did you see the face on the kid behind the front desk?" I ask Carrera.

"It's nice to know I still have my secret powers," she said.

And off we went, in the direction of the setting sun—two grown-ups with lots of hurt and history to put behind us, doing the best we can to move along.

PERMISSIONS

Shorter versions of these stories were first published in:

The Devil and John Holmes: *Rolling Stone*, June 15, 1989
Little Girl Lost: *GQ*, November, 1994
Deviates in Love: *Esquire*, October, 1992
The Porn Identity: *Playboy*, September, 2011

ABOUT THE AUTHOR

Mike Sager is a best-selling author and award-winning reporter. A former *Washington Post* staff writer and contributing editor to *Rolling Stone*, he has written for Esquire for more than thirty years. Sager is the author or editor of more than a dozen books, including anthologies, novels, a biography and textbooks. In 2010 he won the National Magazine Award for profile writing. Several of his stories have inspired films and documentaries; he is editor and publisher of The Sager Group LLC. For more information, please see MikeSager.com.

ABOUT THE PUBLISHER

The Sager Group was founded in 1984. In 2012 it was chartered as a multimedia content brand, with the intent of empowering those who create art—an umbrella beneath which makers can pursue, and profit from, their craft directly, without gatekeepers. TSG publishes books; ministers to artists and provides modest grants; and produces documentary, feature, and commercial films. By harnessing the means of production, The Sager Group helps artists help themselves. For more information, TheSagerGroup. Net.

ALSO BY MIKE SAGER

Non Fiction

Scary Monsters and Super Freaks:
Stories of Sex, Drugs, Rock 'n' Roll, and Murder

Revenge of the Donut Boys:
True Stories of Lust, Fame, Survival, and Multiple Personality

The Someone You're Not:
True Stories of Sports, Celebrity, Politics & Pornography

Stoned Again: The High Times and
Strange Life of a Drugs Correspondent

Vetville: True Stories of the U.S. Marines at War and at Home

The Devil and John Holmes - 25th Anniversary Author's Edition: And
Other True Stories of Drugs, Porn and Murder

Janet's World: The Inside Story of Washington Post
Pulitzer Fabulist Janet Cooke

Travels with Bassem:
A Palestinian and a Jew Find Friendship in a War-Torn Land

The Lonely Hedonist:
True Stories of Sex, Drugs, Dinosaurs and Peter Dinklage

Tattoos & Tequila: To Hell and Back with One of Rock's
Most Notorious Frontmen

Shaman: The Mysterious Life and Impeccable
Death of Carlos Castaneda

Hunting Marlon Brando: A True Story

Fiction

Deviant Behavior, A Novel

High Tolerance, A Novel

THE SAGER GROUP

Artifex Te Adiuva

Printed in Great Britain
by Amazon

79183089R00109